W9-AGU-799

SHAKESPEARE'S SEXUAL COMEDY

A Mirror for Lovers

L ET the love of knowledge be disseminated," cried out the torchbearers; "Not so, but rather the knowledge of love," replied the common man.

George Stewart

HUGH M. RICHMOND

SHAKESPEARE'S SEXUAL
COMEDY

A Mirror for Lovers

822.
33 D
RIC

FINKELSTEIN
MEMORIAL LIBRARY
SPRING VALLEY, N. Y.

THE BOBBS-MERRILL COMPANY, INC.

Indianapolis • New York

72–01718

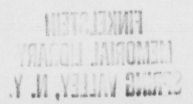

Copyright © 1971 by The Bobbs-Merrill Company, Inc.
Library of Congress Catalog Card Number 77-155437
Printed in the United States of America
First Printing
Designed by Starr Atkinson

Like the love poet Propertius, I dedicate my book
to the Goddess of Good Sense
(if there is one)

Contents

Early Warning   1

I. Shakespeare's Relevance   4

II. *The Sonnets:* Reversal of Expectations in Love   15

III. Sexual Norms Revised   48
     The Comedy of Errors, or the Penalties of Virtue   48
     Love's Labour's Lost: Intellectual Lovers Derided   64
     The Taming of the Shrew, or How a
         Talented Woman Can Become a
         Successful Wife and Be Happy   83

IV. Low Love and High Passion   102
     Bottom as Romeo   102
     Triangles in *The Sonnets* and *The Merchant of Venice*   123
     Rosalind, Helena, and Isabella:
         the Descent to Sexual Realities   137
     Desdemona, and Cleopatra's Escape from Tragic Virtue   158

V. Shakespeare and Modern Sexuality:
     Albee's *Virginia Woolf* and *Much Ado*   177

VI. The Self as Work of Art   197

References   209

Early Warning

ALMOST the twin of my infant daughter, this book was conceived in a Paris flat on the Left Bank, which was soon to reverberate with the echoes of police batons hammering on student skulls and the crash of flying cobblestones. In due course it was born into a Berkeley clouded with tear gas, baptized on Telegraph Avenue in coffee shops flanked by the bayonets of the National Guard, and confirmed in university rooms sprinkled with broken glass or stained by arson attempts. Under the circumstances it is unlikely to prove just another academic book about Shakespeare. The old style of scholarship is manifestly failing to meet certain needs of modern society, while the demand of the young for relevance has led them to reject all but last week's leaders (even Mario Savio looks a bit lonely sitting over there in Cody's bookstore). I find myself dissatisfied with both conventional views; some new synthesis is needed. I am almost tempted to exorcise the demon Confrontation by invoking that fishy British word: Compromise.

A "classic" author who cannot help us to live better now has little claim on our attention; but if there really are any serious young people naive enough to insist that no one over thirty ever said anything relevant to the feelings of the present generation, someone needs to remind them that they are rejecting the only means that will make their aim of cultural reconstruction possible. At least the progressives' need of tradition should be on record. The trouble with most revolutions is that their initiators usually fail to recognize that the word implies a return to where one started (Charles II replaces Cromwell; Louis XVIII, Napoleon;

Stalin, the Tsars; and the new Celestial Emperor Mao revives
the policies of the ancient Ch'in Dynasty). Obviously we cannot
reject the past without becoming its victims; it must be absorbed
to prevent its return on the pendulum swing of the future. That is
why I find the civility of Shakespeare in both political and sexual
affairs more relevant to modern awareness than the cruder manners
of Fromm or Marcuse.

In *Shakespeare's Political Plays* I tried to show his relevance
for people with radical attitudes: if the ill fates of Brutus and
Hotspur are plausible, then we must exile the swaggering ghost
of Ché Guevara to the mythical world of medieval outlaws like
Robin Hood, where it truly belongs. The present essay seeks to
show how naive, archaic, and ineffective are the sexual norms of
both inflexible morality and the so-called "new" freedoms (which
were old-fashioned when St. Augustine wearied of them, not to
mention Byron and Shelley). Berkeley, like every modern university campus, is a bizarre illustration of the failure of the new sexual morality to afford even the minimal social rhythm provided
by repression. It is salutary to evaluate the amatory mysticism of
both a Dante and a D. H. Lawrence in the light of Shakespeare's
final verdict on the sexual cults of Romeo, Othello, and the sentimental heroes of his comedies. Shakespeare shows us that, in love
as in politics, innocent sincerity is not enough; "telling it like it is"
usually shows us only what we wish were true. Shakespeare's comedies suggest to us that men need a higher conception of their
purposes than mere wish-fullfilment provides. They suggest that
we should test high sentiments against the implications of facts
like the daily suicide attempts on my own campus, the five thousand new cases of gonorrhea each day in the United States, and
the collapse of almost all marriages in California between partners
under twenty-five years of age.

Despite my occasional use of it as evidence of how not to
live, I am greatly indebted to the University of California for help
in writing this book. In particular the university's representatives

granted me the time and money which made it possible for me to write at all, a gesture of considerable personal tolerance by my colleagues which I recognize gratefully. Obviously this book also requires more than the usual polite gesture to one's spouse; but while my wife is an essential contributor, I'm sure it will quickly become evident that neither she nor I would wish readers to think it was entirely autobiographical. I also owe my appreciation to all those who have been generous enough to find the project worth encouraging (above all my publisher, Bill Hackett, and a healthy number of people under thirty).

CHAPTER ONE

Shakespeare's Relevance

WHEN the increasing pressure of his own religious convictions made St. Augustine reject his first profession as a "teacher of the liberal arts," he protested that "there is no need for either the buyers or sellers of literary knowledge to cry out against me," for he knew that no man can be more than a clever technician of literary studies without those qualities of character and spirit that ultimately became so important to St. Augustine that he was forced out of the literary profession and into an exclusively religious life. By these standards Ben Jonson, that tirelessly belligerent veteran of so many battles both military and literary, was quite right to stress the personal integrity of "my beloved, the author, Mr. William Shakespeare," when he came to praise him. "I loved the man," he said, "and do honour his memory (on this side idolatry) as much as any. He was indeed honest and of an open and free nature, had an excellent fancy, brave notions, and gentle expressions."

These seem to be the truly sociable virtues Jonson requires of all civilized men, as well as of poets, and they also happily match his view of Shakespeare's literary character. The same ideal of consistency reappears in John Milton's later specification that he who "hopes to write well . . . ought himself to be a true poem." Such testimony explains the special admiration and delight evoked by the career of Shakespeare, whose life seems to display something of the wit and élan which invigorate his writings. We cherish such apocryphal stories as that about the assignation which Shakespeare's friend, the actor Richard Burbage, supposedly managed to make with a beautiful member of his audience, who had been much impressed by his virtuosity in the title role of Richard III, a bravura part created for him by Shakespeare. Shakespeare overheard this arrangement, and himself successfully anticipated the hour of Burbage's amorous visit, feeling that it was really his own due as author; when Burbage later arrived and sent in a message to the lady that "Richard III was at the door," Shakespeare returned the response that William the Conqueror had come before Richard III. The currency of such contemporary anecdotes hints at the liveliness of Shakespeare's reputation as a witty gallant. His provocative literary insights are thus not likely to be false to his own complex experience. He is also clearly not susceptible to the challenge Jonathan Swift threw out against a genteel acquaintance, that he professed to be tender-hearted, but still allowed his coachman to whip his horses. It is difficult not to believe that in handling his own private life, Shakespeare was as deeply responsive and subtle as any of his dramatic characters, and one confidently accepts all his pretensions to human insight. By contrast, it is difficult not to dislike an author like James Joyce precisely because his works affect a humane spirit which is negated by his actual contempt for his associates and the rejection of friends, family, religion, and homeland by which he repudiated humanity itself. Greatness of spirit must surely display the opposite qualities—the willingness in a crisis to sacrifice art to life that was shown by Milton and Swift in their careers, when they turned their literary gifts to serving the political needs of their country and away from purely aesthetic goals. We may recognize that Joyce had the courage of his convictions, that having dedicated himself to art rather than life, he sacrificed himself as well as others to that commitment. But it is hard not to feel that he made the wrong choice and that—despite the instinctive humanity of his feelings for Leopold Bloom and his dislike of Stephen Dedalus' intellectual arrogance—there is something lost in his representation of life as a result of his choice.

In celebrating Shakespeare's virtues I am obviously not praising him for being what unimaginatively conventional people sometimes think of as "moral": pursuing masochistic rectitude and the avoidance of pleasure. After all, one of the greatest of moralists characteristically kept company with whores, thieves, and tax-collectors: he not only excused an adultress and justified a cunning estate manager, but considerately turned his miraculous powers to providing an extra jar of wine when supplies for a friend's feast were running low. Such charitableness both sanctions his authority, and is its goal. Shakespeare shares this acceptance of sensual, earthly life, with all its failures and demands. With apt symbolism his own father appears in history first before a court where he was fined "one shilling for having an unauthorized dunghill in Henley Street." At eighteen, William himself is hastily married to a woman eight years his senior, and their first child is christened six months later. If he runs away from her to London to make his fortune, he finally returns to Stratford, honorably accepting his obligations as husband and father. When William finally dies, legend plausibly ascribes it to the fact that "Shakespeare, Drayton, and Ben Jonson had a merry meeting, and it seems drank too hard for Shakespeare died of a fever there contracted" (John Ward's *Diary*).

Yet this apparent "free liver" was extravagantly compassionate. In his sonnets he seems concerned above all to reconcile himself to the friend who steals his mistress. Needing a spare head to "prove" the decapitation of the sensual young Claudio in *Measure for Measure,* Shakespeare cannot bear even to imagine the execution of a hardened criminal, Barnardine, whom the plot provides to furnish the evidence; he is spared and Shakespeare invents another corpse already conveniently deceased from natural causes. As a young man this compassionate poet might well have been seen crouched down on a bypath waiting for the re-emergence from his shell of a timorous snail frightened by his "tender horns being hit" (*Venus and Adonis,* 1033), or caught momentarily attentive to the emotions of a hunted hare, "poor Wat," whom he happens to glimpse, as the animal

> far off upon a hill,
> Stands on his hinder legs with listening ear,
> To hearken if his foes pursue him still.
>
> (*Venus and Adonis,* 697–699)

When his father's career sinks almost to indigency from the exalted position of mayor of Stratford, Shakespeare takes advantage of his court connections to have a patent of gentility conferred on the old man by the College of Heralds, possibly to compensate for the humiliations of his decline. The playwright's life and works continually suggest this kindliness of vision; even Shakespeare's murderers are still left capable of some insight and humanity, and from Richard III to Caliban, his worst monsters are at least partly redeemed by wit and charm.

Such mercifulness probably explains why Shakespeare was so lovingly remembered seven years after his death that two of his friends labored long and well to collect the many works which he left casually scattered behind him. His unlearned colleagues, John Heminges and Henry Condell, earned the gratitude of all readers of Shakespeare by producing the First Folio, to which every later editor of Shakespeare is largely indebted. Even their innocent prefatory note is valuable for the terms of praise they devote to the plays of their author, terms which have the final authority of simple truth to experience: "We hope, to your diverse capacities, you will find enough both to draw and hold you: for his wit can no more lie hid than it could be lost. Read him therefore, and again, and again. And if you do not like him, surely you are in some manifest danger, not to understand him."

Perhaps this only means that if you dislike Shakespeare, it must be because you are misreading what he has written. But that last sentence suggests something more challenging to me: not to understand and sympathize with Shakespeare's intentions implies that one's mind is sufficiently unbalanced to presage one's own ruin. This, in any event, is the view of Shakespeare which I shall take in this book. Not to have read (or better still, seen) Shakespeare's plays is not merely to miss entertainment and a sense of supreme artistry. It is to risk an impoverished intellectual life, and to invite a ruinous emotional one. There are a few great authors whom one is compelled to use as touchstones to test the worth of one's responses from moment to moment. My own puritanism is tempered by memories of the treatment of sexual freedom in Euripides' *Bacchae,* with its portrayal of the ruin of the "morally responsible" King Pentheus, who represses sexuality only to be destroyed by the explosion of those forces he sought to discipline. Any appreciation of refined sensibility must come to terms with Chekhov's delicate ridicule of the Russian intelligentsia's aspirations to cosmopolitan urbanity, in plays like *The Cherry Orchard* or *The Three Sisters.* The parasitic sophistication of their characters is clearly the prelude to the bloody revolution which is to sweep them into limbo.

For smart young literary critics like Susan Sontag or subtle old magicians like Marshall McLuhan, such naively literal applications put a critic in the class of the simpleton who cries "Watch out!" to the victim in a melodrama. However, one virtue of maturity is the willingness to avow and accept simplicity of mind without equivocation or pretension. We ought to have the courage to reject intellectual fashions when they conflict nakedly with experience, deny the relevance of a man's life and conscious aims to his writing, or fail to recognize that all great literature is a model of reality that serves to suggest how ordinary men can cope with that reality. We cannot wisely reject the goal to which authors like Dante and Milton were explicitly committed: that of saving the souls of their readers. Artistic techniques are certainly necessary to these redemptive campaigns, but ignoring their ultimate ends sterilizes the analysis of great works of literature. This is why the common reader senses that any deep isolation of literature and criticism from life would be false to the originals and irrelevant to his own needs.

The great Anglican theologian of Shakespeare's day, Richard Hooker, once wrote that "the general and perpetual voice of men is the sentence of God himself." Only the enduring response of most ordinary men validates literary excellence, as it does religious truth and political authority. And thus that great English critic Dr. Johnson was right when he felt able to "rejoice to concur with the common reader; for by the sense of readers uncorrupted with literary prejudices, after all the refinements of subtlety and the dogmatism of learning, must be finally decided all claim to poetical honors." It is this common reader who supports the Shakespeare festivals scattered across the United States, even as far as the Pacific Coast—for Californians live at the end of the Western world in every sense, and Shakespeare is the only European author who has made the trip across the Sierras successfully, without turning cranky like most other emigrés. Nevertheless, even he has suffered somewhat: California's Shakespeare often seems to be enormously complicated and even inaccessible if one listens to the professors, or somewhat stiff and tedious on the stage—unless the director has heard of Freud, and then all the actors behave like psychiatric cases, an amusing but scarcely impressive experience for the audience.

But what Shakespeare can achieve in the theater is more important than mere diversion. I remember at Stratford once when an audience of solemn dowagers and innocent bardolaters were so shaken by the first part of *King Lear* that when intermission arrived they not only forgot to applaud; they didn't talk or even move. For a minute or two there was a total silence. Everyone in the theater felt compelled to sit still in order to think urgently how to come to terms with an experience so testing to their moral awareness. Much the same thing ought to be true of the teaching of Shakespeare. He ought not to evoke exclamations over the "beauty" of his verse but remarks like the one I heard from the subdued and rueful voice of experience: "So that's why I got my divorce. . . ." More damage to his work has surely been done by excessively solemn respect for Shakespeare than by crudely inquiring "What on earth is he getting at in this tangle?—and why should I bother about it anyway?" If the only available answers deal with his clever use of oxymoron or his ingenious borrowings from Plutarch or Montaigne, then these answers are falsifying what Shakespeare and his contemporaries expected of drama, and what most popular audiences today find so attractive about his work: a sense of vivid personalities trapped in difficult and fascinating situations which invite us to think creatively about human experience in general, and our own behavior in particular.

These are the kinds of issues which modern Shakespearean critics should be talking about; and unless their work contributes directly to our awareness of the exact nature of Shakespeare's judgments on such crucial matters, most scholars are wasting their time and ours. It is ludicrous to imagine that a man with wits as agile as Shakespeare's has nothing distinctive or decisive to say about politics, or ethics, or any of the other major spheres in which the human mind operates. We have not even started to talk about the essential Shakespeare when we have outlined his use of literary conventions or demonstrated his sources. What we as representative readers must seek are his unique views on the great human issues: love and death, war and revolution, social obligation and human capacity. In books like *The School of Love,* I have already tried to demonstrate that other modern literary creations, comparable to Shakespeare's portrait of Cleopatra, depend on our recognition of an even deeper sense of human nature in its highest and lowest potentialities than that which is reflected in Plato's Diotima or Virgil's Dido. If man cannot learn most pleasurably in this way from the literary records of great minds of past cultures and of his own, literature sinks to mere diversion.

Again I need to stress that I have no naive sense of "learning." I am not proposing that we read the *Agamemnon* Trilogy of Aeschylus to "learn" that it is wicked to kill one's daughter, or husband, or mother. If there are any real moral points to be made about these plays, they are of a more disturbing kind. They suggest that generals who loyally put their public obligations above their family's happiness may pay fatally for their lack of private feeling, when they least expect it; or that the legitimate pangs of affronted mother-love may regrettably ruin a gifted woman who deserves a better fate than to become a murderess; or that well-meaning young men should not accept strong moral imperatives uncompromisingly. Such points are surely not proved to be naive because they can be framed to imply clear admonitions bearing on our own daily behavior. However, some of the subtlest modern literary critics have become so diffident that they find universal virtues chiefly in irony, ambivalence, and ambiguity, ostensibly because they reflect rich and complex awareness. We therefore get Norman Rabkin's claim that *Hamlet* "presents a universe in which we must decide at every moment which way to choose, yet which tells us simultaneously that no choice is possible." Baffled by the difficulty of applying such uncertainties to everyday experience, many general readers still agree with Sir Laurence Olivier's archaic view in his movie that Hamlet's "flaw" lies in his failure to kill Claudius quickly. The idea that any man's deepest moral duty might ever be to get on with a murder expeditiously is so alien to the great religions of the world that merely to consider it as the theme of the play seems the mark of moral imbecility. The plot of the play shows rather the folly of hasty actions of all kinds.

If the modern academic intellectual neglects such recognition of literature's larger bearings, he risks leaving the common reader resentful. In *Paradise Regained* (IV. 322–330), Milton shows Christ denouncing such a critic's state of mind:

who reads
Incessantly, and to his reading brings not
A spirit and judgment equal or superior
(And what he brings, what needs he elsewhere seek)
Uncertain and unsettled still remains,
Deep versed in books and shallow in himself,
Crude or intoxicate, collecting toys,
And trifles for choice matters, worth a sponge;
As Children gathering pebbles on the shore.

Losing larger perspective, the specialized scholar may lose a sense of the general motion of the universe, or even of his own society. He can understand local patterns and movements very well—the kind of thing covered in physics by Einstein's Special Theory of Relativity. But, typically, Einstein's General Theory has never caught on so well; it still lacks broader application and even proof, partly because many modern researchers care less to answer such general questions in most disciplines. Nowadays one rarely asks philosophers about right conduct or the legitimacy of particular values—only about syntax.

Similarly, we have lost the traditional idea that literature should delight *and* instruct: delight its audience in part by instructing them, and instruct them best by wholly delighting them. How many recent studies of classic works of literature convince one of the necessity of carefully reading the books they describe because of their decisive relevance to our daily performance? It is not surprising that many of the students who commit the most violent acts of rebellion these days are students of the humanities. The relevance of geology or even sanitary engineering to the enhancement of modern life may not be morally uplifting, but at least it is unmistakable and demands some respectful attention. But the student who has just heard a two-hour lecture on the irregularity of Wyatt's sonnets, or on Hemingway's syntax, may regrettably purge his boredom and resentment at such irrelevance to his own sense of priorities by burning down the lecture hall, or by forcibly staffing it with people like Eldridge Cleaver who talk about the actual, exciting world of urban America in which people are bribed, raped, and murdered, or become business executives, saints, and politicians. Even among professors there are some who give the most sophisticated lectures yet are themselves dissatisfied enough to favor the mobs in revolt against their own university. As St. Augustine long ago sardonically noted in the *Confessions,* the man who rages over a misplaced comma in the classroom may feel no compunction about raising mass hatreds and violence outside it. Excessive professionalism can lead to such sociological naiveté.

My aim in this book is to try to avoid this mistake by bringing the refinements and discriminations of Shakespeare's genius into closer relation with our own immediate experience, and by relating him to one of the most deeply rooted of our instincts, one governing a significant part of all our daily behavior: sexual desire. My assumption is that Shakespeare's treatment of it may indeed display all the local complexity, irony, relativism, and elusiveness for which he has been praised, but that our residual impression will not be "the impossibility of choice," so much as the unwisdom of harsh actions. Thus I will try to illustrate the scholar-novelist George Stewart's less drastic assertion that "works of literature in general depict individuals who are confronted with the necessity of decisions, that is, of moral judgments." Shakespeare consistently seems to advocate a basic change in his audiences' conventional idealization of sexual love, a skeptical modification sufficiently extraordinary and universal to bear as directly on our own modern behavior as anything in Freud or Fromm—indeed more directly, since the vision rises from a deeper, subtler, and more generous mind than theirs.

My first book, *The School of Love,* was a lovers' handbook in somewhat cowardly masquerade as a scholarly study of western love poetry (a disguise which few penetrated). The present book openly expounds a philosophy of love, with Shakespeare as the mentor, to whom I play a far humbler role than Socrates did to Diotima in the *Symposium.* But the goal remains as broad as their dialogue; it is not primarily to "explain" Shakespeare, but to present his vision of sexual relationships as they might, or even perhaps as they should, be. I expect its argument will provoke disagreement and even resentment, among other reasons because it attempts to break a conditioned reflex of Western man: the excessive idealization of one's lover. But surely this is what all good literary criticism seeks to do: start discussion, not end it.

CHAPTER TWO

The Sonnets: Reversal of Expectations in Love

LIKE other successful dramatists such as Molière, Shakespeare started his theatrical career as an actor, and he may have continued to act at least as late as the first performance of one of his own major tragedies, for Nicholas Rowe suggests that his best role was that of the ghost of Old Hamlet. This professional experience in role-playing may help to explain why Shakespeare seems so conscious of the artificiality of human personality both on and off the stage.

A latecomer to a recent Pirandello revival in New York was asked nervously by those seated next to him, "Are you one of us or one of them?" To Shakespeare this distinction between the roles of the actors and of the audience would have seemed naive. The chief difference would not lie in the fact that one group was acting and one was not. All of them were acting out assumed roles, but each actor knew he was playing a part, while most of the audience would believe that the personalities they had assumed outside the theater were less artificial than those on the stage, not realizing that "All the world's a stage, / And all the men and women merely players," as Jaques observes in *As You Like It* (II. vii. 139–140).

At the heart of Shakespeare's art lies this recognition that any confidence about personality is based only on a willful and dangerous delusion of consistent identity. The plots of most of his plays derive from the grotesque consequences of taking one's own supposed nature too seriously. And nothing proves worse than the natural propensity for visualizing oneself as really well-meaning—unless it be the expectation of consistent behavior from others with as worthy a view of themselves, for this is what ruins Othello and Desdemona, Lear and Cordelia. Shakespeare's truly experienced characters are more like Benedick, who accepts his evolving identity for the "giddy thing" it is at the end of *Much Ado* (V. iv. 109). Modern situation ethics says much the same thing, telling us that there are no "bad" or "good" people, only fortunate or difficult situations. The wise man simply refuses to be permanently trapped in any disastrous set of attitudes, which for Shakespeare usually means one reinforcing our sense of our own worthiness.

A startling example of this view of maturity appears in Shakespeare's sympathetic presentation of the evolution of the deposed Richard II, whose mental growth is reflected in his enhanced capacity to imagine alternative roles for his lost one of king, to which he had too confidently committed himself. Richard mitigates the distress of his imprisonment with the aid of this new imaginative flexibility, sharing Jaques' vision of personality when he recognizes that "thus play I in one person many people" (V. v. 31). Richard's earlier lack of this faculty for switching personae is what distinguishes his own youthful failure as a king from the later success of the supple Prince Hal, who finally inherits Richard's throne. Before his own accession Hal has been subtly trained to accept the elusiveness of identity by his experience of the witty affectations of Falstaff, and of the various deceptive "coats" which insure his father's safety (*1 Henry IV,* V. iii, iv). Such flexible natures as Hal's compel Shakespeare's fearful admiration, as he testifies in Sonnet 94:

> They that have power to hurt and will do none,
> That do not do the thing they most do show,
> Who, moving others, are themselves as stone,
> Unmoved, cold, and to temptation slow,

> They rightly do inherit heaven's graces
> And husband nature's riches from expense;
> They are the lords and owners of their faces,
> Others but stewards of their excellence.

As a moral ideal this temperament may at first sight seem questionable, if not hypocritical; but its essential trait lies in the freedom of such personalities from total surrender to the roles required of them. Outwardly they appear sincere and committed enough to convince those with whom they have to deal, yet they never exploit their reserves of inner detachment to harm those who trust them. The sonnet asserts that God favors those capable of such skeptical commitment; I intend to argue that Shakespeare shows us that only lovers attaining this kind of detached yet participating role can maintain a mature relationship, and that the failure to recognize these interacting values has impaired the worth of our ideals of sexual relationships.

The *Sonnets* are an excellent place to begin because they are written from the point of view of a speaker fully endowed with Shakespeare's own power over words and insight into people's minds. Generations of scholars have failed to separate the "I" of the sonnets from Shakespeare himself. Indeed Frances Meres, acting as a kind of Elizabethan gossip columnist, asserted that the *Sonnets* were intended only for "private friends." This seemed to be confirmed when their surreptitious publication in the first edition of 1609 was efficiently suppressed, presumably by some national figure powerful enough to prevent their historical content from interfering with his career. In explanation of how this edition appeared at all, John Dover Wilson recently assumed that Shakespeare's own private collection of copies of the first 126 sonnets was stolen for a publisher who had purchased the remainder of the cycle from the files of the scandalous and mercenary Dark Lady, to whom they are mostly addressed. If this theory is correct, there must have been an explosive amount of historical truth locked up in the cycle: even the publisher of the next complete edition (in 1640, twenty-four years after Shakespeare's death) found it advisable to alter several of the poems to obscure the relationships involved.

However, the autobiographical precision of the poems is less important as history than as the source of their plausibility and depth as poetry; for no man writing sonnets is under oath to tell the exact truth, particularly if he exploits the traditional sentimental themes of the sonnet form as cleverly as Shakespeare. What is important is that here we have the presentation of the amatory encounters of an extraordinary pair of Elizabethan gallants, quite free of the stage and plot limitations of theatrical comedy or tragedy. Shakespeare is under no pressure here to retell the borrowed stories of his amatory plays, with their frequent remoteness of time or place. These sonnets do not deal with Cleopatra's Egypt, or Othello's Cyprus, or a mythical Venice, or Verona. They are set in Shakespeare's London, and the protagonist's experience is as immediate and historically plausible as Casanova's accounts of his loves in his *Memoirs,* or those of Rousseau and Frank Harris in their confessions. This is how a personality (or even a mere persona) endowed with faculties like Shakespeare's might plausibly respond to the tensions of love and friendship.

The first thing that startles the reader about the sonnets is the emotional virtuosity of the protagonist. The poems appear to have been composed over a longer period of years, and to cover a greater range of passionate experience, than any one of the plays. In recognizing the variety of moods and attitudes Shakespeare accumulates in the sonnets, we may choose either to admire his protean nature as an actual passionate friend and lover, or to stress his dexterity in accumulating such an extraordinary range of amatory motifs from literary sources. Either his own nature was unusually flexible and susceptible, or he deliberately chose to display the full scope of literary permutations of which emotional relationships are capable. Probably both views are true: he dexterously coordinated first-hand experience with the accumulated resources of the sonnet tradition, from the solemn and sentimental to the cynical and outrageous.

The speaker begins the cycle in a complacently paternal mood: the mature man of the world counsels his gifted junior to achieve immortality for his attributes by begetting children on the body of a complaisant wife. Beauty requires sexual intercourse to sustain itself from one generation to the next. Thus, unexpectedly, copulation proves to be an aesthetic obligation for the handsome and beautiful; it preserves their charms for posterity's admiration. However, the somewhat sententious tone of these opening sonnets to a young male friend contrasts startlingly with the frank avowals of the speaker's own promiscuous heterosexuality in the last sonnets, like 150, 151, and 152. With candid, if fairly tactfully phrased detail, he confesses that his irresistible physical response to the presence of his sinister mistress defies all his moral and psychological discriminations:

> For, thou betraying me, I do betray
> My nobler part to my gross body's treason;
> My soul doth tell my body that he may
> Triumph in love; flesh stays no farther reason;
> But, rising at thy name, doth point out thee
> As his triumphant prize. Proud of this pride,
> He is contented thy poor drudge to be,
> To stand in thy affairs, fall by thy side.   (151)

These physiological facts override all other, more intellectual considerations: the awareness of the adultery of which both are guilty, even the fickleness of the woman. Indeed, the tangle of dishonored relationships in which both are involved defies mathematical computation:

> In loving thee thou know'st I am forsworn,
> But thou art twice forsworn, to me love swearing,
> In act thy bed-vow broke and new faith torn
> In vowing new hate after new love bearing.

> But why of two oaths' breach do I accuse thee,
> When I break twenty? I am perjured most;
> For all my vows are oaths but to misuse thee
> And all my honest faith in thee is lost.   (152)

Shakespeare here makes clear that for a lover to protest devotion and constancy in a vicious relationship merely perverts the participants in it further: to praise a woman for her skill in adulterous lovemaking merely insults and debases her by stressing her commitment to amorality. The ultimate corruption in this particular relationship comes when the mistress progresses beyond delight in adultery, and even beyond willful fickleness to her new companion. Now she no longer even bothers to satisfy the speaker's sexual demands, yet still contrives to excite his perverse delight in this humiliating phase of their relationship:

> Whence hast thou this becoming of things ill,
> That in the very refuse of thy deeds
> There is such strength and warrantise of skill
> That, in my mind, thy worst all best exceeds?   (150)

In such poems, Shakespeare dexterously plots the lowest levels of sado-masochism with no less authority than he had earlier plotted the opposite extremes of idealizing emotion. His speaker savors the delights of torment with convincing appreciation of the expertise with which they are administered by a woman cleverly attuned to his practiced tastes.

Have we really gained so much insight through the recent crudely physiological descriptions of a modern eroticist like Pauline Réage in the *Story of O,* when Shakespeare has already mapped out the psychological range of these perverse relationships so much more fully and accurately? For the startling thing about the sonnets is that, while they portray the depravities of love—its antisocial, psychologically destructive phases—yet, unlike most modern pathologies of sexuality, they do so in forms that coexist with, even require the contrast of, the most sublime moments of human ex-

perience: the ecstasies of friendship, of aesthetic and moral idealism, and of defiance of the fatal mutability of the universe by an
all-enduring human will. Very few authors can measure as accurately as Shakespeare such differences in mood and yet remind
us of the essential interdependence of conflicting statements, like
those in 106 and 129:

> When in the chronicle of wasted time
> I see descriptions of the fairest wights,
> And beauty making beautiful old rhyme
> In praise of ladies dead and lovely knights,
> Then, in the blazon of sweet beauty's best,
> Of hand, of foot, of lip, of eye, of brow,
> I see their antique pen would have express'd
> Even such a beauty as you master now.　　　　(106)

The capacity for such ecstatic appreciation must be bracketed with
its vicious doppelgänger, the inevitable recessive phase of the
manic-depressive cycle, so familiar in Shakespeare's major
tragedies:

> The expense of spirit in a waste of shame
> Is lust in action; and till action, lust
> Is perjured, murderous, bloody, full of blame,
> Savage, extreme, rude, cruel, not to trust,
> Enjoy'd no sooner but despised straight,
> Past reason hunted, and no sooner had
> Past reason hated, as a swallow'd bait
> On purpose laid to make the taker mad;
> Mad in pursuit and in possession so;
> Had, having, and in quest to have, extreme;
> A bliss in proof, and proved, a very woe;
> Before, a joy proposed; behind, a dream.
> 　　All this the world well knows; yet none knows well
> 　　To shun the heaven that leads men to this hell.　　(129)

Such a juxtaposition must suggest to us that only a mind
capable of the idealistic praise of a friend in the earlier sonnet could

rage so bitterly at the humiliatingly bestial effects of sexual desire
in the later one. The later sonnet is less graceful because of its harsh
tone and destructive impact on the reader's mood. But it is an
essential corollary of "Shall I compare thee to a summer's day?"
or "Let me not to the marriage of true minds / Admit impediments." As we can see in *Timon of Athens,* only a persona susceptible to these extravagant moods of commitment and philanthropy
is plausibly capable of such vitriolic fury at the emotional shock of
human failure: Timon cannot endure Athens's contempt once he
has exhausted his resources for the sake of his friends, and he seeks
the city's annihilation. On one level such sentimental extremes are
the phases of a mind not fully in control of itself. Timon becomes
a misanthrope, switching personae as involuntarily as Othello does
when his extravagant love for Desdemona's purity turns to hate for
her supposed depravity, or as Lear does in abruptly turning against
his favorite daughter, Cordelia.

These wild swings of attitude are therefore not accidental.
It is in this sense that the cycle seems to be truly dramatic: in its
comprehensiveness and its endless capacity for providing illuminating juxtapositions of varying responses to intense relationships.
These add up to a total effect vastly different from the impact of
many of the most admired single sonnets. The basic dramatic pattern shifts the reader's attention from poems like the extreme ones
just quoted toward others, rarely celebrated for their beauty or art,
which nevertheless reflect a state of mind free of the excesses both
of adulation and of despair, to which the delicate sensibilities of
the speaker are all too prone. This is why the primarily autobiographical approach to this poetry is shortsighted. If we consider
the sonnets as simply a lively but haphazard kind of autobiography
we shall miss their complex and calculated contrasts of feeling.
This counterpoint gives the sequence its coherence and its value
for us as a comprehensive map of passion whose value far exceeds
the interest of a series of titillating "revelations" into which Shakespeare was accidentally betrayed. With this sense of the cycle as a

comprehensive poetic model of the phases of deep passion, I think we shall be a little less anxious to find out whether the elusive Dark Lady really was Mrs. D'Avenant, or the friend was the Earl of Pembroke. Even the idea of a story (whether fictional or not) becomes marginal to our concern with understanding the consistent nature of passion. Such a reading of the sonnets may seem somewhat alien at first to any modern reader who tends still to expect the tidy patterns of a well-told tale, not the discontinuous exploration of the various levels of an enduring but complex social and psychological situation.

I do not mean that the sonnet cycle lacks a progression; rather, that progression does not depend on our concern to learn the outcome of a sequence of external events, but on our excitement at the clarification of an interlocking set of passionate relationships and the way they are sustained. Such objective events as the betrayal of the speaker's trust by the affair between his friend and his mistress are more important because they help to define latent aspects of the relationships than because they change them in any ultimate way. All deep attachments must meet and survive such shocks. The "story" can thus be briefly summed up in all its limited essential details in a mere few lines of a late sonnet, 144:

> Two loves I have of comfort and despair,
> Which like two spirits do suggest me still:
> The better angel is a man right fair,
> The worser spirit a woman colour'd ill.
> To win me soon to hell, my female evil
> Tempteth my better angel from my side.

This is the essential triangle of emotional forces, and there is no resultant, no clear final outcome for the "plot" which would seem to resolve the tensions in terms of a basic alteration in the relationship such as the end of the friendship, or the rejection of the mistress. Indeed, even the opening sonnets of the cycle already seem to suggest a casualness in the young friend's attention to the speaker's concern for his virtue. His later susceptibility to the Dark Lady's distracting influence is implicit in the young man's neglect of his friend's advice to use his own best resources significantly and not in pursuit of inferior goals.

So that if there is drama in the cycle, it does not involve many decisive changes in the outward relationship; it derives from our surprise in recognizing the full nature and consequences of intense involvement with another human being. However, the recognition of some of these factors, once established, may prove irreversible. In this sense the relationship does evolve and mature: the speaker does not openly abandon either his friend or his mistress, because he finds new modes of thinking which sustain the relationships so that they are less subject to extreme (not to say terminal) responses. If there is a significant sequence it is not a chain of changing relationships—friendship, attachment, betrayal, reconciliation—but the development of the art of avoiding such a cycle. Some critics have even argued that a first, insignificant mistress, involved in the earlier poems only, is seduced by the young friend, and that the later poems about the Dark Lady relate to a second liaison of the speaker's, in which this time it is the older woman who seduces the young friend. Surprisingly, the possibility of so radical a divergence of plot does not touch the profoundest sequence of feeling in the cycle, for it displays the final maturing of the speaker's power to handle the complex tensions and tangles of *any* combination of intense attachments without betraying himself into the suicidal inanities of a Romeo or the murderous moods of Othello. This is why the sonnets are so important: they afford a "sentimental education" of the subtlest and most creative kind.

From this perspective the much-debated question of the sonnets' correct sequence appears largely irrelevant. Since they plot some of the wide range of permutations possible in passionate attachments, almost any juxtaposition is revealing. Indeed, the cycle affords a far better opportunity for a rewarding shuffle of its component parts than Burroughs's fashionable modern novels, where

we are told that the order of each set of pages can be endlessly re-
arranged to provide new insights. Each Shakespearean sonnet significantly modifies our response to any other with which it is read
in close conjunction. The relative banality of 54—

> O, how much more doth beauty beauteous seem
> By that sweet ornament which truth doth give!

—can only be fully savored if it is read with 138:

> When my love swears that she is made of truth
> I do believe her, though I know she lies,
> That she might think me some untutor'd youth,
> Unlearnèd in the world's false subtleties.

Obviously in the latter sonnet the speaker has now attained some
of the skeptical dexterity merely described earlier, in 94, though
the situation is amusingly complicated by the fact that his sexual
partner is no less agile in 138:

> Thus vainly thinking that she thinks me young,
> Although she knows my days are past the best,
> Simply I credit her false-speaking tongue:
> On both sides thus is simple truth suppress'd.

In these three poems we are confronted with a startling spectrum
of possible amatory attitudes: the vision in 54 of innocent truth on
both sides (which *Romeo and Juliet* and *Othello* prove to be disastrous); skeptical flexibility by one partner, as in 94 (the starting
point of most of the comedies, as we shall see); or, in 138, mutual
skepticism (which is the key to Shakespeare's greatest romance,
Antony and Cleopatra).

　　Most young lovers in my classes favor the first option, with
uniformly ludicrous if not tragic results (only one youthful marriage in seven now survives in California). They often become
very angry when I warn them that they haven't a chance unless at
least one of them is skeptical about the other's worth and virtue.

One pair in one of my courses got married enthusiastically after a few meetings, skipped class while I was teaching *Romeo and Juliet* and *Othello,* got separated after confusions comparable to those of Shakespeare's lovers, and were able to take my final examination on these plays having lived through comparable experiences well enough to do brilliantly on the finals. It seems a rather exhausting way of developing sexual awareness and not very convenient as a substitute for the full range of literature, though we do see the same kind of desire for first-hand experience in the present disturbances among many humanities students (who seem bent on fighting the monsters of *Beowulf* in the streets, or experiencing *War and Peace* on their own campuses). It is extremely hard but absolutely essential for their survival to encourage such independent spirits to gather experience vicariously through empathy with literary figures like the protagonist of the *Sonnets*. It is a challenge to every responsible teacher and critic that no modern young undergraduate can readily believe with Donne that "The Ecstasy" of the moment can be confining and foolish, if not fatal; and that the best he can ultimately hope for sexually is Shakespeare's wry conclusion to his speaker's self-questioning in Sonnet 138:

> But wherefore says she not she is unjust?
> And wherefore say not I that I am old?
> O, love's best habit is in seeming trust,
> And age in love loves not to have years told:
> Therefore I lie with her and she with me,
> And in our faults by lies we flatter'd be.

The condition of the lovers presented in this poem is Shakespeare's highest wisdom on the subject of sex, and the best literary model available for an enduring relationship between man and woman. The other great literary love affairs are all unconsummated, like Dante's cult of Beatrice, or ruinous, like most "great" love stories. Perhaps some lovers do need the added excitements of their own and others' ruin to heighten their sexual satisfactions, wishing that they too could bring about a national disaster like the wreck of Arthur's court achieved by Guinevere's romantic attachment to Lancelot, or the international holocaust precipitated by Antony and Cleopatra. Obviously readers who sympathize with such love of picturesque disaster should study Shakespeare, who vindicates the skeptical commitment of the last sonnet quoted as the inescapable condition for a lover who wishes to sustain his relationship. Indeed, this state of mind becomes the psychological ideal of all Shakespeare's sexual comedy.

However paradoxical it may seem, this also is the kind of disillusioned vision that a few later wits of almost Shakespearean subtlety have further developed, and none more disturbingly than Swift when he harshly rephrased his master's insight in *A Tale of a Tub:* "For, if we take an Examination of what is generally understood by Happiness, as it has Respect, either to the Understanding or the Senses, we shall find all its Properties and Adjuncts will herd under this short Definition: That, it is a perpetual Possession of being well Deceived. . . . If this were seriously considered by the World, as I have a certain Reason to suspect it hardly will; Men would no longer reckon among their high Points of Wisdom, the Art of Exposing weak Sides, and publishing Infirmities; an employment in my Opinion, neither better nor worse than that of Unmasking, which I think, has never been allowed fair Usage, either in the World or the Play-House. . . . He that can with Epicurus content his Ideas with the Films and Images that fly off upon his Senses from the Superficies of Things; Such a Man truly wise, creams off Nature, leaving the Sower and the Dregs, for Philosophy and Reason to lap up. This is the sublime and refined Point of Felicity, called, the Possession of being well deceived; The Serene Peaceful State of being a Fool among Knaves." The value of the *Sonnets,* in contrast to this point of view, lies in the exposition of how to accept such a role consciously and gracefully in love, a thing we know Swift was largely incapable of conceiving or practicing.

Perhaps so harsh a truth cannot be assimilated in its raw Swiftian state; but I trust the general reader to find its vindication in the multiplicity of picturesque analogues and models for actual experience evident in Shakespeare's works. Nowhere more vividly than in the *Sonnets* can we see the inevitability of the reduction of whole-hearted commitment to something like skeptical devotion. Let us begin by recognizing that two more gifted men could hardly be evoked than the speaker and his friend in the *Sonnets*. The speaker has been held to possess all the talents of Shakespeare, and the friend is so fascinating that even the classic betrayal of stealing a mistress does not impair his attractiveness. Shakespeare goes to such extreme lengths in detailing the extraordinary endowments of the two men that we may be the more inclined to believe that these unusual creatures cannot have been invented. It seems more likely that Shakespeare is illustrating the old saying that "truth is stranger than fiction," thus implicitly bypassing Aristotle's dictum in his *Poetics* that poets should prefer the probable to the possible when choosing materials for their fictions.

Obviously we are also not dealing simply with conventional courtship and flattery, even though the sentimental literary resources of the sonnet tradition are elaborately exploited throughout the cycle. The exact shade of emphasis in the opening sonnets advocating marriage can only be explained by postulating the very specific situation of an older acquaintance (with some intellectual advantage but lower social standing) advising a gifted young aristocrat to accept his social and biological role; the speaker seems to be motivated in his counsel by a concern for the young man's family. That this situation has a remarkable precision helps to explain why literary scholars are so encouraged to look for appropriate parallels in the lives of men like the future Earl of Pembroke, in the last years of the sixteenth century. However, I would also stress that the arguments in these sonnets are analogous to those which Falstaff brings to bear against the younger Lancastrian princes (such as Hal), with their calculating aloofness to emotional involvements. In both cases, the arguments rise quite naturally from a more or less historical context, yet their interest transcends any actual historical derivation.

What makes the speaker of the opening sonnets such a useful norm against which to measure the narrower mind of a Romeo or an Othello is this universality, the superiority of the speaker's motives to the usual selfish concerns of a sonnet writer. Many love poems had argued for sexual intercourse as a necessary part of the cosmic cycle, but most had done so to betray a young beauty into her lover's bed. Few had done so in the cause of marriage, and still fewer to insure the marriage of the beloved to someone else. Far from raising the question of homosexuality (rejected for its physical limitations, in language of deliberate bluntness, in 20), the opening group of sonnets displays a unique relationship, and a unique vision of passion which is ultimately at odds with the pre-eminently idealistic, Neoplatonic tradition that dominated much of Renaissance amatory poetry.

The *Symposium* had argued for Love's supreme egotism in his "designs upon the beautiful," in which he must prove to be "a master of device and artifice, ... an adept in sorcery, enchantment, and seduction." The selfish motive lies in the fact "that Love longs for the good to be his own for ever." Unexpectedly, Diotima does provide some precedent for Shakespeare, when she recognizes that the urge to seek immortality lies behind much sexual desire: "This is how every mortal creature perpetuates itself; it cannot, like the divine, be still the same throughout eternity; it can only leave behind new life to fill the vacancy that is left in the species by obsolescence. This, my dear Socrates, is how the body and all else that is temporal partakes of the eternal; there is no other way. . . . Those whose procreancy is of the body turn to woman as the object of their love, and raise a family in the blessed hope that by doing so they will keep their memory green, 'through time and through eternity.' " Nevertheless, Diotima decides that "the beauties of the body are as nothing to the beauties of the soul." Marriage is thus the inferior choice for a would-be lover.

It is precisely this preference which is missing from the opening sonnets of Shakespeare's cycle. The speaker is practically concerned to preserve the beloved's genetic resources, not to progress through admiration of his exquisite physique to that spiritual awareness of beauty in general which is favored by Diotima. Yet Diotima had asserted that physical procreation is motivated by an egotistical desire for self-perpetuation, while love for another member of one's own sex tends toward a higher spiritual motivation, because physical propagation is denied to it. Obviously Shakespeare manages to produce a totally different emotional configuration in his attitude to his young friend, while using the same range of ideas as Diotima. His tone remains idealistic, yet his primary concern is with the temporal world and marriage, not with philosophic transcendence. Only in the immortality to which his art aspires does the speaker expect to have some personal compensation.

Shakespeare thus seems to present us, in the opening sonnets, with an eminently un-Christian approach to the world, one which favors aesthetic over moral values and inherited advantage over actual performance. The superior individual is idealized as a kind of secular incarnation of the excellent; most of his personal activities are incidental (perhaps even irrelevant) to his mere existence as a uniquely admirable object. Nevertheless, these first sonnets are not lacking in emotional refinement and that kind of discriminating intellectual awareness solicited by Diotima. Far from striving to dominate and isolate his beloved as Socrates insists in the *Phaedrus* that the baser kind of lover will, the speaker in the early sonnets advocates the transmission of his beloved's excellences for the benefit of others, and particularly through the taking of a wife. The speaker's motives are not narrowly personal, nor are they even paternal—the young man will serve not so much his own good as society's in enlarging his intimacy to embrace a wife.

This concern with the public good is both extraordinary in amatory verse and eminently Shakespearean. It is a powerful positive note on which to open our reading of the sonnets; and the characterization of the personalities involved is unusually positive in other ways also. The speaker shows a superiority to the selfish claims of love which would be improbable and forced if its occasions were not so dramatically varied—from the philoprogenitive marriage sonnets to the pensive moods of those that confront the dual failures of the two men in their relations with both the fickle mistress and the rival poet. Yet if the speaker shows an extravagant unselfishness in all these complications, the character of his friend seems positively superhuman: its virtue survives every failure in a way which rounds out this extraordinary personality through dramatic contrasts and confrontations largely missing in the presentation of such impassive dames as Dante's Beatrice, Petrarch's Laura, Sidney's Penelope Devreux, or Spenser's Elizabeth Boyle. It is this range of incident and particularity which makes the total impact of the *Sonnets* more dramatic than lyric. Instead of the simple, lyric idealization of the beloved mistress characteristic of earlier sonnet cycles, which progress only from subjective enthusiasm to despair or disillusion, Shakespeare's sonnets build up the friend as a unique yet realistic character who gives solidity and plausibility to a superiority of temperament which earlier lyricists had merely asserted, usually without conviction or historical substance (no one else among their contemporaries seems to have noticed its existence). Again, as with the protagonist, one is tempted to seek the historical foundations of Shakespeare's cycle as the key to his elaborately realized portrait of the friend, which exceeds the bounds of fancy and the merely "probable" that Aristotle had urged on poets.

According to Clarendon's *History of the Rebellion,* the relevant Earl of Pembroke was indeed such a superior man. In his maturity he attained great "fame and reputation with all men, being the most universally loved and esteemed of any man of that age. . . . And as his conversation was most with men of the most pregnant parts and understanding, so towards any who needed support or encouragement, though unknown, if fairly recommended to him, he was very liberal. And sure never man was planted in a Court that was fitter for that soil, or brought better qualities with him to purify that air. Yet his memory must not be so flattered that his virtues and good inclinations may be believed without some allay of vice, and without being clouded with great infirmities, which he had in too exorbitant a proportion. He indulged to himself the pleasures of all kinds, almost in all excesses. Whether out of his natural constitution, or for want of his domestic content . . . he was given up to women. But therein he likewise retained such a power and jurisdiction over his very appetite, that he was not so much transported with beauty and outward allurements, as with those advantages of the mind as manifested an extraordinary wit and spirit and knowledge, and administered great pleasure in the conversation. To these he sacrificed himself, his precious time and much of his fortune. And some who were nearest his trust and friendship were not without apprehension that his natural vivacity and vigour of mind began to lessen and decline by these excessive indulgences." Thus even in maturity this man gave rise to anxieties about the use of his gifts comparable to those aroused by his earlier resistance to marriage (which make him such a plausible candidate for the role of the young friend in Shakespeare's sonnets).

My point is not that Pembroke *must* be the friend but that Clarendon's account of him proves the plausibility of the uniquely gifted personality evoked by the speaker in the sonnets. We know for a fact that such men as Pembroke were among those personally intimate with Shakespeare; they inevitably provided traits not only for the figure of the friend in the sonnets but also for such brilliant and assured characters in the comedies as Biron, Petruchio, and Benedick. Yet in the sonnets the ultimate effect of the presentation of such a gifted personality and of his friendship with a poet whose genius is so akin to the author's is by no means reassuring in its implications. The medieval tragic view of fortune (which survives in the modern aphorism, "the higher they come, the harder they fall") is amply corroborated by the evolution implicit in the cycle. An extraordinary tension develops between the reader's sense of the excellence of the two friends and his recognition of the recurrent failure of the relationship to sustain the high expectations it naturally arouses. And this is not to be explained by the intrusion of the baser temperament of the symbolically dark Lady.

In his moments of recrimination, the protagonist is less concerned with betrayal by his mistress than with the potential decline in his relationship with the friend:

> That thou hast her, it is not all my grief,
> And yet it may be said I loved her dearly;
> That she hath thee, is of my wailing chief,
> A loss in love that touches me more nearly.   (42)

The probable failure of what has seemed an ideal of friendship reminds us that from the start the very perfection of the young man has implied problems—in the first instance a narcissistic self-sufficiency, which is now reflected in an indifference to the feelings of even his close acquaintances. Beauty fails to function socially in the opening sonnets because of its own complacency; and in the theft of a friend's mistress this social limitation of excellence is further realized, in ways that the psychologist Adler was to rationalize far later: the gifted and the beautiful lose in sensitivity because they need to make so little effort to win others' devotion. The cycle's speaker must thus confront the dangers implicit in any man's mental and physical gifts, and the resulting impairment of confidence in the possibility of enduring human bonds between the best of men. Finally, he even has to recognize not only his friend's necessary limitations but also the destruction of his own narcissistic satisfaction in the eternal fame promised by his poetry. Precisely because both men are so finely endowed they prove more prone to disaster than humbler men, who seem likely to have more need to avert it.

For in Sonnet 18 his opening movement had struck a self-confident balance between his friend's gifts and his own art:

> And every fair from fair sometimes declines,
> By chance or nature's changing course untrimm'd;
> But thy eternal summer shall not fade
> Nor lose possession of that fair thou owest;
> Nor shall Death brag thou wander'st in his shade,
> When in eternal lines to time thou growest;
>   So long as men can breathe or eyes can see,
>   So long lives this and this gives life to thee.

Even at this stage, the poet's apparent vainglory conceals a valid psychological awareness. There is a compensatory element in his proud assertions, for through them some kind of mutuality with the aristocratic friend becomes possible, and without such a sense of equivalence no human relationship is truly viable. Yet in due course we see the poet confronted with the failure of this aesthetic ideal which gives him status as the purveyor of preservation for the individual identity, a role in which he had hoped to replace with his verses the immortalizing progeny the young man refuses to beget. Ironically, the poetry fails as the friend does; poetry cannot "immortalize" mortal men without falsification.

A whole series of sonnets seems to document the failure of such aesthetic immortality when it lacks the substantial content of an active relationship:

> O, how I faint when I of you do write,
> Knowing a better spirit doth use your name,
> And in the praise thereof spends all his might,
> To make me tongue-tied, speaking of your fame!   (80)

The poet discovers that he cannot rival the artistic virtuosity of his competitors with their "new-found methods" and "compounds strange" (76). He complains that "true plain words" fail before such "strained touches" of their rhetoric (82), and in 87 he wakes

from his dream that the most gifted men can discriminate between
his own true art and the mere virtuosity of his rival:

> Farewell! thou art too dear for my possessing,
> And like enough thou know'st thy estimate:
> The charter of thy worth gives thee releasing;
> My bonds in thee are all determinate.
> For how do I hold thee but by thy granting?
> And for that riches where is my deserving?

But the mere fact of the decline in the relationship is not the whole
story. Other poets have built their careers on such distress, but
Shakespeare is unusual when he shows his speaker asserting that
great art cannot be built out of such deprival and failure. Involved
in a valued relationship, Shakespeare's art supposedly could confidently meet this rival's poetic challenge:

> No, neither he, nor his compeers by night
> Giving him aid, my verse astonished. . . .
>   But when your countenance fill'd up his line,
>   Then lack'd I matter; that enfeebled mine.   (86)

No longer can Shakespeare's speaker find security in his own
unsupported literary talents; without truly inspiring content, art
is insignificant.

The speaker's next resort for sustaining the crumbling relationship is his own humility, his acceptance of whatever role the
survival of his friendship requires. There is at least some satisfaction in the virtuosity with which he submits himself totally to the
humiliations required by this minimal accord with his beloved:
he pretends to share the contemptuous view of his own character
adopted by his friend. Some kind of accord seems possible in Sonnet 88, even if it must lie in the censure of a false personality pro-
jected onto the speaker:

> When thou shalt be disposed to set me light
> And place my merit in the eye of scorn,

> Upon thy side against myself I'll fight
> And prove thee virtuous, though thou art forsworn.
> With mine own weakness being best acquainted,
> Upon thy part I can set down a story
> Of faults conceal'd, wherein I am attainted,
> That thou in losing me shalt win much glory: . . .
>> Such is my love, to thee I so belong,
>> That for thy right myself will bear all wrong.

The acceptance of so self-destructive a role in the interest of the beloved is less perverse than it might seem. It illustrates a climactic attempt to equalize the balance between the two men: even in self-censure, Shakespeare's speaker seeks to demonstrate that he is his friend's superior. His censure of himself is more effective than the attacks of those who have repudiated his friendship. And his capacity to achieve this bitter self-confrontation on behalf of his beloved illustrates a devotion surely scarcely to be surpassed. Very few lyric love poets have been able to accept this final role convincingly, and even fictional parallels are mostly post-Shakespearean (Dmitri Karamazov's acceptance of another's guilt being one of the nearer parallels in moral temper).

Yet the sonnet sequence does not even leave the situation there, with a moral victory of sorts for Shakespeare's speaker. His almost Christlike acceptance of guilt and shame on behalf of those he loves contains the potentiality for a final humiliation that leaves him stripped of all virtue and dignity. In Sonnet 88, the speaker had not merely accepted the role of a legitimately rejected acquaintance: his absolute innocence had been qualified by the admission that he himself could find *actual* faults, unrecognized by others, but which he admitted as good grounds for the rejection. The ultimate humiliation latent in this concession is revealed in Sonnet 109, and those following it. The speaker is now cast in the worst part of all, one which is no longer an assumed role but based on the notorious fact of his own viciousness:

> Alas, 'tis true I have gone here and there
> And made myself a motley to the view,
> Gored mine own thoughts, sold cheap what is most dear,
> Made old offences of affections new;
> Most true it is that I have looked on truth
> Askance and strangely.   (110)

It might be argued that the failures here seem more intellectual or social than moral or criminal. They are such as Shakespeare himself might avow to an aristocratic patron, if financial pressures forced him to take to the road again in his old unfashionable role as an actor, or if he had used knowledge of their intimacy to flesh out some of his material for his still all-too-humble career as a playwright (say, in the profane Hal-Falstaff scenes, or the positively debauched Bertram-Parolles ones). However, other sonnets go beyond the suggestion of such mere tactlessness, indecorum, or emotional betrayal. The reader must register the ominous implications against the speaker when he mentions the accusation that he may have been "false of heart" (109); or admits a "strong infection" leading to "harmful deeds," from which his name "receives a brand" (111); or ruefully laments the "vulgar scandal stamp'd upon my brow" (112).

This theme of failure nevertheless serves as the foundation for the construction of a more resilient ideal of love, which has survived to this day in triumph. One good reason for accepting the coherence of the present arrangement of the poems lies in its juxtaposition of these rueful admissions of failure and perhaps the most famous sonnet in the whole sequence, 116:

> Let me not to the marriage of true minds
> Admit impediments. Love is not love
> Which alters when it alteration finds,
> Or bends with the remover to remove.

The conventional response is to read this as a simple lyric state-

ment, an unqualified positive assertion of the speaker's own commitment. Nevertheless, its customary context in the sequence suggests how we might interpret Sonnet 116 rather differently and
far more personally than traditional readings allow. Its heightened
intensity and passion rise not from the speaker's sense of his own
worth and ideals, since he has shown in the sonnets immediately
preceding that he has failed to maintain these. His goal is thus not
self-assertion, but the desperate need to find a logic of love which
will free him from the legitimate punishment for his public failures: his own repudiation by his friend. The dramatic context of
116 thus requires us to understand it not as saying: "How magnificent my love is: I can forgive anything you've done, and even
the fading of your beauty." (When this situation occurs, the tone
is far more plaintive and negative, as in Sonnet 40.) What he is
really saying is: "I hope that you are as superior an individual as I
think, for then you will confirm my trust in our relationship and
not hold my present failure against me—any more than I will
blame you for the fading of your beauty."

The change in application involved in this reading is central
to my view of the *Sonnets*. It displays how completely love requires
that we discard our image of our own worth and capacity if we
are to get along with the complacent censures of a person sufficiently well endowed to invite our devotion. If falling in love is to
be more than a casual experience, lovers must expect and resolve
their inevitable and painful misunderstandings. Even more, they
must learn to accept the painful consequences of the genuine failures which Adler asserts to be the inevitable penalties of any major
virtues or graces with which lovers may be endowed. It may be for
this reason that many men of genius seem to have married older,
ugly, or harsh-seeming women: Socrates did, even Petrarch, Shakespeare himself, Balzac, and many more. The manic Italian genius
Torquato Tasso said in one of his poems "About Beauty" that a
beautiful mistress was a disaster; he wanted a nice, ugly, older

woman who would be grateful for any love at all and who would be proportionately tolerant of her lover's failures and humble about her own.

This illustrates the self-discipline needed by aspiring lovers, which Shakespeare's speaker learns by accommodating himself to the perfections of his friend. Very early he recognizes that his own nature exposes him to the threat of justified criticism by his friend, and in Sonnet 49 he makes a first desperate gesture of humility to forestall that awful moment:

> Against that time, if ever that time come,
> When I shall see thee frown on my defects, . . .
> When love, converted from the thing it was,
> Shall reasons find of settled gravity,—
> Against that time do I ensconce me here
> Within the knowledge of mine own desert,
> And this my hand against myself uprear,
> To guard the lawful reasons on thy part:
>> To leave poor me thou hast the strength of laws,
>> Since why to love I can allege no cause.

Here for once we may identify in Shakespeare the full force of anti-humanist Christian dogma; the speaker accepts St. Paul's warning that "No man can justify himself before God by a perfect performance of the Law's demands" (Rom. 3:20). Ironically, Paul feels that this awareness is the prelude to a sense of God's mercifulness: Shakespeare's speaker seems to hope for similar good will from his friend by surrendering any egotistical complacency about his own worthiness, as he makes another lover observe in *Love's Labour's Lost* (IV. iii. 67): "Thy grace being gain'd cures all disgrace in me."

It is a testimony of the agility of Shakespeare's mind that he accurately presents the corollary of this hope for the beloved's tolerance of manifest defects in the lover: the comparable need for the speaker's own tolerance of extreme failures on the part of the beloved. While lacking God's supposed self-sufficiency (which theologians argue is adequate to the forgiveness of all mortals without strain), Shakespeare's speaker nevertheless struggles ingeniously to rationalize even the worst of betrayals (as in Sonnet 40) so that he will not feel constrained to resent it to the point of "altering" his love:

> That thou hast her, it is not all my grief,
> And yet it may be said I loved her dearly;
> That she hath thee, is of my wailing chief,
> A loss in love that touches me more nearly.
> Loving offenders, thus I will excuse ye:
> Thou dost love her, because thou know'st I love her;
> And for my sake even so doth she abuse me,
> Suffering my friend for my sake to approve her.   (42)

It is immaterial that the argument does not seem to convince even the speaker; he is vindicated not by the particular devices of rationalization which he invents but by the purpose of the attitude he is supporting by these specious arguments. His view is that conscious participation in a valued relationship can be effectively maintained in the face of

> reckoning time, whose million'd accidents
> Creep in 'twixt vows and change decrees of kings,
> Tan sacred beauty, blunt the sharp'st intents,
> Divert strong minds to the course of altering things.   (115)

Consider how different the actual behavior of a lover truly committed to an enduring relationship is from that of one merely protesting eternal devotion. The self-deceiving idealist glories in his own devotion, but his very self-confidence allows him promptly to find good reasons for breaking off the relationship, as we shall see Claudio doing in *Much Ado*. The discriminatingly committed soul recognizes that a friendship or a love affair can be made to endure only by an enormous intellectual effort, a profound acceptance of humiliation, and a capacity to endure the apparent failure even of the beloved. Perhaps such an acceptance of disadvantages will appear contemptible to those who have been conditioned to stand firmly on their rights. The acceptance of unfair treatment is neither very American nor indeed very human, but suave acceptance is the only mature and civilized response to maltreatment, at least in private life, and perhaps in public too. Violent resentment of human failure is always the mark of stupidity.

Certainly, if one expects nothing but good from society (as even minority groups are led to expect and therefore demand in the United States), then the inevitable failures lead to violent resentment and suicidal despair. We find all too many dreamers of "the American dream" (which surely ought not to fade so rapidly when accurately paraphrased as "the American myth"), who wake to the harsh realities of life only to share the mood of Shakespeare's speaker in one of his least viable states: "Tired with all these, for restful death I cry, . . . from these would I be gone" (66). Such a mood leads to murder and self-destruction, whether one's name is Othello or Hamlet or a more contemporary one. Expectation of good is the prelude to violence, and often misdirected violence, as any child psychologist can tell you.

Expect the best of love and you will necessarily bring about the worst. The dangers of the use of rigorous judgment in love need little exposition: Shakespeare's plays are full of deliberately extreme illustrations of them. But the sonnets outline the issues more economically and thus can serve explicitly as an introduction to the analysis of *Othello* and other plays. One consideration in avoiding judgments of one's lover is the elusiveness of proof of something so intangible as alienation:

> Thou mayst be false, and yet I know it not.
>
> So shall I live, supposing thou art true,
> Like a deceived husband; so love's face
> May still seem love to me, though alter'd new;

> Thy looks with me, thy heart in other place:
> For there can live no hatred in thine eye,
> Therefore in that I cannot know thy change.   (92–93)

The further complication is that even seemingly substantial "evidence" in love affairs is rarely of true legal standing, a fact which Othello does not recognize but the sonnets' speaker does. Indeed Sonnet 70 goes even further and asserts that malicious rumor may well direct itself rather at the innocent than the corrupt:

> That thou art blamed shall not be thy defect,
> For slander's mark was ever yet the fair;
> The ornament of beauty is suspect,
> A crow that flies in heaven's sweetest air.
> So thou be good, slander doth but approve
> Thy worth the greater.   (70)

In such a context of confusion and deception it is not surprising that the fraudulence of most divorce-court evidence provides corroboration of the impossibility of "proving" responsibility and guilt in these intangible sexual relationships. As California law has at last come to recognize, the crucial evidence for divorce is not technical adultery or wildly inflated acts of "cruelty" but the fact that at least one of the partners does not want to make the effort necessary to continue the relationship. Shakespeare shows us that it is at least conceivable for a lover to accept anything from his beloved if he chooses to rationalize away the difficulty. And indeed in many cases the evidence for a lover's repudiation is no more valid than Othello's excuse for murdering the innocent Desdemona. The speaker in the sonnets reaches full recognition of this in his summary of the cycle's plot in 144:

> To win me soon to hell, my female evil
> Tempteth my better angel from my side,
> And would corrupt my saint to be a devil,
> Wooing his purity with her foul pride.

And whether that my angel be turn'd fiend
Suspect I may, yet not directly tell;
But being both from me, both to each friend,
I guess one angel in another's hell.

The result of such awareness of uncertainty is the justification for those complex personalities praised in Sonnet 94, "that do
not do the thing they most do show." Obviously one cannot hope
to maintain that any personality will consistently reveal itself in the
best light in love affairs, nor that total trust can plausibly be sustained in one's inmost heart. The merely skeptical mutual tolerance already described in 138 is the inevitable condition of a sustained relationship. Indeed, one of the more ominous signs in any
sexual relationship is likely to be the absence of misunderstandings
which need to be ingeniously overcome; such absence of tension
may indicate not idyllic compatibility but cynically systematic cov-
ering-up. This is surely the psychological implication of the prover-
bial "calm before the storm," and the partial explanation of Shakespeare's famous phrase in *A Midsummer Night's Dream* (I. i. 134):
"the course of true love never did run smooth." If you are getting
on too effortlessly well with your wife or mistress she's probably
deceiving you, or planning a divorce.

Such a view of love naturally provides a further, moral di-
mension for the unattractive beloved favored by Tasso. An ugly
mistress is more trustworthy and responsive; one whose faults you
know is more reliable than one who can disguise her limitations:

In the old age black was not counted fair,
Or if it were, it bore not beauty's name;
But now is black beauty's successive heir,
And beauty slander'd with a bastard shame:
For since each hand hath put on nature's power,
Fairing the foul with art's false borrow'd face,
Sweet beauty hath no name, no holy bower,
But is profaned, if not lives in disgrace.   (127)

It may not be accidental that this late sonnet should be the first detailed allusion in the cycle to the attributes of the Dark Lady, as if we were now seeing applied to a specifically sexual relationship the lessons learned from the tensions of the passionate friendship with the exquisite young man. Progressing from the cult of the outwardly perfect, Shakespeare is now committed to the pursuit of the frankly blemished. He is not merely reconciled to the Lady's aesthetic and moral limitations, he is positively reassured by them. In a certain sense, black becomes beautiful for him.

The last twenty-eight sonnets in Shakespeare's cycle are more nearly Christian than the others, if Christianity means (as I believe it does) the acceptance of the need and value of loving the imperfect and incomplete. The Christian rejects the vaingloriousness of Plato and his followers, who believe we should rationally love only what is better than we, spurning inferiors while we ourselves aim to become like gods. Man, to a Christian, is necessarily finite, lacks omniscience, and therefore must fail in most of his endeavors. This is the nature of man in the universe, a fact we must recognize, but for which we are not to be blamed or penalized theologically as long as we do not foolishly try to talk others or ourselves into believing the contrary. The relief derived from this sense of cosmic tolerance for admitted failure allows us to be comparably merciful to those who fail as we do. And this is how Shakespeare comes to present the most mature moods of his sonnet cycle. The speaker's commitment to his friend and his mistress may inevitably have wavered, but it has never been abandoned. It starts as a doomed secular religion of the beautiful, but evolves to a Christian sexuality and a Christian friendship, in which it becomes possible to live with one's own perverse nature and that of one's intimates without getting permanently neurotic about it. Christianity in these terms might be paraphrased as "everyone has hang-ups about something; the best thing to do is to accept them quietly and make the most of what's left over."

Shakespeare's devotion to the Dark Lady takes precisely this view of love; it seeks no delusive ecstasy but accepts the worth of a sexual relationship with someone less than divine, that is, like most women:

> My mistress' eyes are nothing like the sun;
> Coral is far more red than her lips' red;
> If snow be white, why then her breasts are dun;
> If hairs be wires, black wires grow on her head.
> I have seen roses damask'd, red and white,
> But no such roses see I in her cheeks;
> And in some perfumes is there more delight
> Than in the breath that from my mistress reeks.
> I love to hear her speak, yet well I know
> That music hath a far more pleasing sound;
> I grant I never saw a goddess go;
> My mistress, when she walks, treads on the ground:
>   And yet, by heaven, I think my love as rare
>   As any she belied with false compare.   (130)

The poem rejects the technique of praise which the earlier, more idealistic sonnets had used to flatter the young man At least in sexual relationships, such comparisons are now seen to be normally the result of the viewers' own exalted personal moods, not just the product of their beloveds' actual, probably mediocre natures. Shakespeare's speaker sustains a sexual relationship devoid of such conventional lovers' illusions. His mistress is not extravagantly gifted, but nevertheless she is no worse than the most exalted of women, whose worth is likely to be little better for their lovers' praises. Thus, after all, the Dark Lady proves comparable to Beatrice and Laura and other celebrated females. Furthermore, the poet does not need to falsify her nature in order to remain her lover. Indeed, it is quite possible to read the concluding couplet not just as a negative compliment ("She's no worse than the most praised women really are"), but as a positive commitment ("Though skeptical about extravagant praise, I find my beloved as distinguished as the most celebrated of women").

The sonnet cycle reaches its ultimate point of amatory sophistication in such poems. In them the lover's traditional sentimental persona is ruthlessly evaluated, its delusions shown and rejected, its advantageous commitment recognized and maintained. Most lovers unconsciously exaggerate the excellence of their mistresses in order to justify their own allegiance; Shakespeare shows how that allegiance can plausibly be sustained by a personality closely resembling his own, without delusion, by consciously playing the part best suited to sustaining the love affair. Life becomes the dexterous manipulation of graceful contrivances to sustain love: "Love's best habit is in seeming trust" (138). What maintains an enduring sexual relationship is thus an honorable kind of role-playing, refined in this case to a high art, in which each lover gains reassurance from the apparent good will, restraint, and deliberate allegiance of the other partner, in spite of their known defects and any occasional lapses from such a purely artificial, contrived identity on both sides:

> Therefore I lie with her and she with me,
> And in our faults by lies we flatter'd be.   (138)

It is an ideal of love surprisingly compatible with Christian ideals: "Judge not, that ye be not judged. For with what judgment ye judge, ye shall be judged: and with what measure ye mete, it shall be measured to you again." So Matthew quotes Christ, in his seventh chapter, as Shakespeare will recall in *Measure for Measure*.

Of course, conventional modern Christians accept the need for this suppression of judgment all too rarely, and precious few accepted it earlier. Everywhere across the United States (not to mention churches in Europe) we find so-called Christian clerics cursing and judging almost everybody within earshot, which in this electronic age means almost everybody. As Sir Thomas Browne once dryly said, if all Christian judgments were approved by heaven, no Christians would ever get there. So perhaps in proposing that Shakespeare's apparent ideal of sexual relations in the *Sonnets* is loyalty to one's beloved with such deliberate forbearance in the face of defects as human nature can attain, I am ascribing to him an ethic the world is unlikely to entertain very sympathetically, at least on the evidence of simple assertion. It is for this reason that Shakespeare's plays are so valuable to us. The *Sonnets* illustrate the evolution of a sexual ethic in a single, vivid sexual triangle. The plays display almost endless permutations of sexual relationships as seen from the point of view outlined in the sonnet cycle. The ultimate state of mind of the speaker in the *Sonnets* may indeed appear intolerable at first sight to a "sincere" or even to a civilized modern lover. But as we go through the plays it should become clear that the only likely alternative to the wise hypocrisy of the mature sonnets is a disastrous failure in love whose outcome must be either extravagant comedy or fatal violence. The newspapers are full of accounts not only of the divorces but also of the violent deaths of young people unnerved by the ludicrous sexual and moral norms of our overrational society, as with the resentful young idealist who gunned his girl friend down in the Berkeley university library recently. Every day at least one attempt at suicide occurs on my campus alone, mostly because of excessive idealism. If the ideals of Western lovers remain Lancelot, Tristan, a misrepresented Romeo (reincarnated in *West Side Story*), and the like, these psychological disorders will increase. Our current sexual ethic is essentially medieval, and about as adequate as the flat-earth cosmology of that age is to our present geographical needs. Shakespeare is one of the few authors to present a plausible and coherent alternative, with vivid dramatic illustrations of his point. I intend to show that he does not hold up Romeo for our admiration but for our pity. His amatory ideals are Petruchio with his shrew Katharina, or Benedick and Biron with theirs, and a host of other witty skeptics whose view of their beloveds approximates the clown Touchstone's wry satisfaction at the conquest of the rustic wench, Audrey: "a poor . . . ill-favoured thing, sir, but mine own" (*As You Like It,* V. iv. 61). I do hope my female readers can be convinced that this is the ideal attitude to solicit in their suitors: avowed loyalty without illusions.

CHAPTER THREE

Sexual Norms Revised

"THE COMEDY OF ERRORS"

OR

THE PENALTIES OF VIRTUE

M ARRIAGE has traditionally had little to do with passionate love or even simple sexual satisfaction. In this the institution perhaps reflects St. Paul's most limiting trait, his lack of any deep personal respect for sexual relationships, either in physical or in emotional terms. Medieval experts in courtly love were delighted at the opportunity afforded by this rejection of amatory experience to heighten sexual excitement by opposing it to the mediocre satisfactions allowed in "holy" matrimony. One medieval authority, Andreas Capellanus, illustrates the effects of the orthodox view of marriage: "I am greatly surprised that you wish to apply the term 'love' to that marital affection which husband and wife are expected to feel for each other after marriage, since everybody knows that love can have no place between husband and wife. . . . For what is love but an inordinate desire to receive passionately a furtive and hidden embrace." The modern "Anglo-Saxon" prejudice in favor of marrying one's beloved seems to have become fashionable around Shakespeare's time, when its characteristics were illustrated by a series of eccentric writers: Spenser actually had the "bad taste" to marry the woman to whom he addressed his sonnets, and Milton later affronted contemporary religious thought by arguing that sexual and psychological compatibility was a primary consideration in any marriage, and that its lack might be a ground for divorce. Everyone at that time knew that divorce was unnecessary, because custom decreed that emotion had nothing to do with marriage. Inevitably, Milton was greeted with a storm of abuse and by the suppression of his work, a response which encouraged him to write *Areopagitica* in defense of freedom of the press. However, he was later reconciled with his own fugitive wife, and thus lost interest in both issues, ultimately becoming Cromwell's press censor.

Shakespeare's own erratic marital career may have similarly focused his attention on the moral and sexual issues raised by such aberrations; one of the principal subjects in his plays is eccentric marriage relationships. His writings are full of idealistic husbands and fiancés misguided enough to be sentimentally in love with their wives or to marry their beloveds, but these obtuse males usually end by murdering, abandoning, or generally mistreating the women as a result of their own idealism. The women, in turn, usually go to truly fantastic lengths to dominate the men, even if they reciprocate their suitors' affections. Putting a deceived husband or lover into bed with a woman he does not want is just one characteristic little trick for combating male intransigence to which two of Shakespeare's more pious heroines resort. Shakespeare has a knack for picking up stories which contain such extraordinary sexual tangles. *The Comedy of Errors* is a case in point: it depends largely on Plautus's tragicomedy *Amphitryon,* which deals with the irritating problem of what to do if your priggish wife unwittingly allows herself to be debauched by your double during your absence from home as the commander of a successful military campaign. The fact that she was previously pregnant and that your elusive double appears to be the King of the Gods, Jove himself, further complicates the situation. The correct response to this fantastic situation proves, of course, to be to do nothing. And when Amphitryon's son is born he turns out to be

Hercules. It is a very confusing situation, but not without its compensations for Amphitryon.

Moreover, the husband's ambiguous position is similar to that of the speaker in the *Sonnets* in that little substantial evidence of guilt is available, and in that Amphitryon's wife has betrayed her husband unintentionally. Indeed, a modern psychologist might see the play as a dexterous illustration of the way in which the magnificent figure of a victorious general becomes independent of his private personality, so that even his wife copulates with that "divine," imagined hero-image, rather than with the body of her far less dazzling husband, victorious though he may be. Shakespeare takes the theme of this startling tragicomedy and characteristically sweetens, complicates, and rationalizes it. The wife ceases to be pregnant; she is not even imaginatively betrayed into adultery; and she is contrasted with a sensible sister, Luciana, whose love affair serves as a foil to the marriage problems of the somewhat too serious-minded wife, Adriana.

Moreover, Shakespeare borrows many farcical complications from another, merrier Plautine comedy of mistaken identities, *The Maenachmus Twins*. A modern audience confronted by the confusions of Shakespeare's two sets of identical twins may properly be skeptical about the surface realism of the play, but it has its own kind of plausibility: people's identities do shift as the play seems to show them shifting. Schizophrenia involves two or more minds in one body, as with the doppelgängers and doubles in works like Stevenson's *Dr. Jekyll and Mr. Hyde*, or *The Three Faces of Eve*. The dazed general Amphitryon is thus properly warned by his servant: "You're Amphitryon, all right. But be careful: the way people have been changing ever since we got back, you might lose your right title to it if you don't watch out." What we have in all the confusions in these works is not simply a quaint excuse for the thin plot a farce needs. The bizarre happenings permit a systematic attack on the solidity of conventional personality: most of the characters in Shakespeare's play find that their status and identity are

largely dependent on what other people believe them to be. The
attempt by Antipholus of Syracuse to reunite his long dispersed
family is thus not simply a plot contrivance but the pursuit of a
psychological coherence between his subjective self and his social
environment:

> He that commends me to mine own content
> Commends me to the thing I cannot get.
> I to the world am like a drop of water
> That in the ocean seeks another drop,
> Who, falling there to find his fellow forth,
> Unseen, inquisitive, confounds himself:
> So I, to find a mother and a brother,
> In quest of them, unhappy, lose myself.
>
> (I. ii. 33–40)

For the city of Ephesus is very curious in its disintegrating
impact on such volatile strangers. It regretfully condemns to death
Ægeon, the father of Antipholus, the instant he arrives, for violat-
ing a ban on citizens of his state. And because it already houses
Antipholus's own brother, it greets his twin from Syracuse with a
confident familiarity which proves as stupefying as any of General
Amphitryon's experiences, and thus justifies the visitor's own
expectations:

> They say this town is full of cozenage,
> As, nimble jugglers that deceive the eye,
> Dark-working sorcerers that change the mind,
> Soul-killing witches that deform the body.
>
> (I. ii. 97–100)

Again the modern audience may choose to put this situation down
to mere poetic fancy; but there is historical evidence that Ephesus
actually was a place where weird goings on were common. In the
Acts of the Apostles, the city is noted both as a great commercial
center and as a place of pagan pilgrimage to the famous shrine
of the many-breasted Diana of the Ephesians. It also provided

the setting for some of St. Paul's most hallucinatory miracles, mostly healings of schizoid mental conditions, which were so much discussed that they affected the trades dependent on the pagan cult of Diana. The native witches and magicians were converted en masse to the new psychiatry, much to the indignation of the exploiters of the local tourist trade, who feared for their sale of art objects to the previously pagan pilgrims. As usual on his missionary travels, Paul was thus maneuvered into a legal confrontation with the local Establishment over the issue of law and order. However, when the matter was presented to an Ephesian magistrate, it was handled with exceptional discrimination. The justice recognized that one could hardly punish someone for correcting personality disorders: among other things, there could be no substantial evidence in such mental cases, a fact that remains convenient to psychiatrists in court to this day. So the magistrate dismissed the case, advising the plaintiffs to restrain their resentment, just as Jove advised Amphitryon: "Men of Ephesus . . . you ought to be calm and do nothing rash. For you have brought these men here who are neither guilty of sacrilege nor blasphemy. . . . We are even in danger of being accused of riot over today's uproar, since there is no culprit whom we can hold liable for this disorderly gathering."

Shakespeare thus shows his usual superb tact in making Ephesus the setting for his investigation of the bearing of legal evidence and judgments on amatory states—precisely the problem that makes most modern divorce cases so totally ridiculous. And Shakespeare's Ephesus again proves itself to be accurate in judgment yet merciful in practice, by allowing the doomed Ægeon a little time to try to find a bondsman willing to put up bail to save his life. The city also shows that it is traditionally experienced in handling psychiatric cases: when Antipholus of Ephesus begins behaving eccentrically as a result of the actions of his as yet unknown twin from Syracuse, the resort to systematic Pauline therapy is prompt if somewhat extreme, as we see in Dr. Pinch's treatment:

> I charge thee, Satan, housed within this man,
> To yield possession to my holy prayers
> And to thy state of darkness hie thee straight:
> I conjure thee by all the saints in heaven.   (IV. iv. 57–60)

Unfortunately, Dr. Pinch is no St. Paul: the result of the exorcism in the play is identical to the effect of Paul's unskilled Ephesian imitators in Acts. In one such case, "the evil spirit answered, 'Jesus I know, and I am acquainted with Paul, but who on earth are you?' And the man in whom the evil spirit was living sprang at them and overpowered them all with such violence that they rushed out of the house wounded, with their clothes torn off their backs."

Evidently one may not achieve much by being solemnly pious about other people's crazy behavior. Indeed, under the circumstances, the resentment of Antipholus at his wife's attempt to declare him lunatic is entirely plausible. Her judgment of his mental condition is comically misinformed: she blames him for actions of which he is completely unaware. We know that she is so incapable of accurately observing the man with whom she is emotionally involved that she cannot even tell when his apparent body is governed by another personality: his twin's. When the unmarried Antipholus happens to visit her, she simply does not notice that he is not her husband. Since such outrageous failures in discrimination may seem impossible nowadays, it is worth recalling the recent case described in pretty detail by all the national newspapers, in which a respectable man living with his wife and family in the Midwest was astonished to find himself claimed as her husband by a woman whom he appeared genuinely not to recognize at all. The states of mind of the amnesiac and his two irritated wives have taken a great deal of painful medical and legal effort to disentangle, and their loss of focus has a lot in common with that of the victims of the confusion in Shakespeare's *Comedy*.

Most of the play's characters find their moral, emotional, and legal expectations perpetually affronted by the incredible behavior

of those they love and trust, behavior which seems like that of crim-
inals or lunatics. Ægeon thinks he has encountered the son whom
he raised in Syracuse; but far from being saved by his son Ægeon
is cruelly abandoned to his fate, for the person he has met is actually
the lost son, who cannot identify him (perhaps another analogue
to classic neurosis thrown up by the plot). It is not surprising also,
after his mistreatment by his wife Adriana, that this same son
should, in his turn, haul that wife up before the tribunal and
howl for

> Justice, sweet prince, against that woman there!
> She whom thou gavest to me to be my wife,
> That hath abused and dishonour'd me
> Even in the strength and height of injury!
> Beyond imagination is the wrong
> That she this day hath shameless thrown on me.
>
> (V. i. 196–202)

No one likes being treated like a lunatic, particularly by his own
wife.

On the other hand, of course, Adriana did intend his treatment for the best: she really thought she had solid grounds for
incarcerating her husband. As in the sonnets, everyone *means* very
well, and precisely because they are so conscientious, the tangle
seems to get worse and potentially more tragic. *The Comedy* is one
of Shakespeare's most interesting plays precisely because he shows
how disorder can originate without villains simply because everyone professes the very best of intentions. All the characters are
loving, and yet they contrive to maltreat and misjudge those they
profess to love. The ethics that govern their responses are shown
to be not so much "good" or "bad" as irrelevant to the experiences
with which they are confronted. Above all they are inadequate to
resolve the complicated situations resulting from the interaction
of sexual desire and the usual human falsifications of personal
identity, which may be accidental or deliberate.

In all these misunderstandings Adriana is the figure most obviously relevant to the experience of modern American women. She is intense, committed, and intellectually active. Modern readers will sympathize far more than the Elizabethans with her resentment at the way men are unfairly favored by society's double standard:

> Why should their liberty than ours be more? . . .
> Look, when I serve him so, he takes it ill.
>
> (II. i. 10, 12)

Her vision of marital communion includes our modern expectation of psychological compatibility, which was first analyzed by Milton's divorce pamphlets (an ironic omen if ever there was one). Nothing could appear more admirable than Adriana's approach to her alienated husband:

> How comes it now, my husband, O, how comes it,
> That thou art thus estranged from thyself?
> Thyself I call it, being strange to me,
> That, undividable, incorporate,
> Am better than thy dear self's better part.
> Ah, do not tear away thyself from me!
> For know, my love, as easy mayst thou fall
> A drop of water in the breaking gulf
> And take unmingled thence that drop again,
> Without addition or diminishing,
> As take from me thyself and not me too.
> How dearly would it touch thee to the quick,
> Shouldst thou but hear I were licentious . . .
> Wouldst thou not spit at me and spurn at me . . .
> I know thou canst; and therefore see thou do it.
> I am possess'd with an adulterate blot; . . .
> For if we two be one and thou play false,
> I do digest the poison of thy flesh.　(II. ii. 121–146)

The complete spiritual communion that Adriana here requires in marriage had for the most part previously been considered ap-

propriate only to extramarital sexual liaisons such as that of
Petrarch and Laura or Dante and Beatrice (all of whom had
families of their own), or to homosexual friendships of the
kind favored by the men in Plato's *Symposium* (which evolved
into the Renaissance ideal of friendship illustrated in the
Sonnets).

The *Sonnets* already have shown us the inadequacy of this
attractive vision of spiritual communion as a basis for enduring
friendship and even for sustained adultery. *The Comedy* illustrates
its incompatibility with both a workable marriage and a meaningful courtship. Adriana's husband, for example, is from the start
far from delighted to have a doting wife; "My wife is shrewish,"
he says ruefully (III. i. 2). Similarly, her sister feels that Adriana's
sexual intensity is largely pernicious in practice; Luciana attacks its
symptoms as "self-harming jealousy" (II. i. 102). However, the
worst feature of any sentimental commitment of a deeply subjective kind is that the loss of objective awareness makes the lover
project a false image on the behavior of others, to the confusion of
everyone. Adriana is quite incapable of accurately observing her
own behavior or of considering her husband objectively. She is so
sure of herself that when a man resembling her husband visits her
house she is not aware enough of his actual identity to notice that
he is not her husband; sentimental people see only what their own
emotions anticipate. Moreover, after entertaining a mere stranger
as her husband, Adriana goes on to accuse that husband of intended
incest and accomplished adultery, because the visiting twin brother
had taken advantage of his bachelorhood to court her sister Luciana
and to respond to other advances than Adriana's own.

Nowhere is there a more poignant illustration of the pernicious consequences of high sexual expectation than the effect of
Adriana's obtuseness on her real husband. Locked out of his own
home by his well-meaning wife, Antipholus first plans to break
in and create a scandal, but then decides:

>   I will depart in quiet,
> And, in despite of mirth, mean to be merry.
> I know a wench of excellent discourse,
> Pretty and witty, wild and yet, too, gentle:
> There will we dine. This woman that I mean,
> My wife—but I protest, without desert—
> Hath oftentimes upbraided me withal:
> To her will we to dinner.   (III. i. 107–114)

The result of Adriana's high standards is thus that she locks herself up in her home with a "husband" who appears to her an incestuous debauchee and encourages her true spouse to take the first positive steps toward effective adultery. As in politics, so in love: the idealist provokes the exact opposite of his desires.

Adriana's idealism almost ruins her marriage, leading her to incarcerate her husband and drive everyone with whom she is associated into a condition of near frenzy. This is what comes of taking one's social roles seriously; and the validity of this general view is confirmed by the misadventures of the unmarried twin whom she mistakes for her husband. He unwittingly goes along with her fantastic mistakes because his personality is similar to Adriana's. Both treat life with deep seriousness, which means that they get involved in endless confusions and disasters. Believing their sentimental fantasies are objective truth, they make no effort to grasp the complex relativism that governs all significant human relationships. Antipholus of Syracuse goes one stage further: disgusted by Adriana's "lunatic" sexual advances, he is, by contrast, fascinated by her sister's paradoxical coldness toward him as a potential suitor. Since she hesitates to become involved emotionally with her supposed brother-in-law, her impassivity affords the perfect blank screen on which a sentimentalist like Antipholus can project his own sexual fantasies. A responsive mistress would, like Adriana, rapidly generate confusions; so Antipholus understandably follows the traditions of courtly love and pursues a mistress who appears to be totally indifferent to him. (Traditionally, frigidity has always been an ideal attribute in such a sentimentalist's mistress; she should be neither promiscuous nor responsive, merely impassive, if he is to indulge his egotistical delusions without shocks. This is why most sentimental poets' women seem nonentities to the judicious reader.)

Like most idealizing suitors, Antipholus approaches his mistress in a dazzled state of mind which openly fails to grasp the social and psychological factors involved in the relationship. Probably only naive persons fall in love unreservedly, and the wisely cool-tempered individuals (like Luciana) to whom they are attracted accept them because wisdom denies the discriminating beloveds this total commitment, yet makes them merciful to the self-deceivers capable of it. Thus almost every successful love affair is essentially a compromise between a simpleton whose naive commitment makes it possible and a cunning skeptic wise enough to tolerate such a lover yet clever enough to steer them both clear of the disasters which befall idealistic lovers involved with others not unlike themselves, such as Romeo and Juliet, or Othello and Desdemona. Fortunately Luciana and the unmarried Antipholus twin are lovers of the complementary rather than this identical kind, which augurs a final happy outcome for their relationship. Antipholus frankly admits in the midst of his courtship of her that he has not the faintest clue about his beloved's identity, or even his own:

> Sweet mistress,—what your name is else, I know not,
>   Nor by what wonder you do hit of mine,—
> Less in your knowledge and your grace you show not
>   Than our earth's wonder, more than earth divine.
> Teach me, dear creature, how to think and speak;
>   Lay open to my earthy-gross conceit,
> Smother'd in errors, feeble, shallow, weak,
>   The folded meaning of your words' deceit.
> Against my soul's pure truth why labour you
>   To make it wander in an unknown field?

Are you a god? would you create me new?
Transform me then, and to your power I'll yield.

(III. ii. 29–40)

Antipholus totally fails to apply commonsense to his amatory situation, and that failure immediately proves likely to destroy the possibility of a significant relationship with the woman he reverences (because of her supposed insight, which is actually the result of purest coincidence). From awe at her knowledge of things he happens to share with Luciana's brother-in-law, Antipholus swings to terror at the sense of his own crumbling identity in the face of his beloved's enigmatic authority. Lacking real understanding of their sexual relation, his passion oscillates madly between love and fear:

There's none but witches do inhabit here;
And therefore 'tis high time that I were hence.
She that doth call me husband, even my soul
Doth for a wife abhor. But her fair sister,
Possess'd with such a gentle sovereign grace,
Of such enchanting presence and discourse,
Hath almost made me traitor to myself:
But, lest myself be guilty to self-wrong,
I'll stop mine ears against the mermaid's song.

(III. ii. 161–169)

Obviously the lover is unaware of what was so authoritatively portrayed in the *Sonnets*: the inevitable self-betrayal in any intense relationship. His egotistic complacency comes close to destroying the love affair even before it begins.

By contrast, the skeptical, even cynical discriminations of his beloved Luciana suggest a mind unwilling to make drastic and irreversible choices and capable of contemplating human viciousness without hysterics. She warns Adriana against overreaction to her "husband's" lapses, taking the *Sonnets'* view that love implies trust and humility: "Ere I learn love, I'll practise to obey" (II. i. 29). In her response to the proposals of Antipholus she displays a fascinating poise, despite as complete an unawareness of the actual situation as anyone else in the play. It must be remembered that it appears to her that her brother-in-law is trying to get her to go to bed with him, at the cost of her own chastity as well as of her sister's trust. It is precisely the kind of situation that would move an idealist like Adriana (or Othello) to moral, not to say homicidal, fury. Luciana's wry, self-revealing response to all affronts is admirable for its precision, tact, good sense, and modest candor. She counsels the supposedly erring husband to show at least an outward loyalty to his wife, whatever his real motives:

> for her wealth's sake use her with more kindness:
> Or if you like elsewhere, do it by stealth;
>   Muffle your false love with some show of blindness:
> Let not my sister read it in your eye;
>   Be not thy tongue thy own shame's orator;
> Look sweet, speak fair, become disloyalty;
>   Apparel vice like virtue's harbinger;
> Bear a fair presence, though your heart be tainted;
>   Teach sin the carriage of a holy saint;
> Be secret-false: what need she be acquainted?
>   What simple thief brags of his own attaint? . . .
> Alas, poor women! make us but believe,
>   Being compact of credit, that you love us;
> Though others have the arm, show us the sleeve;
>   We in your motion turn and you may move us.
>
>   (III. ii. 6–16, 21–24)

One sees at once the parallel here to the wry description of the affair with the Dark Lady given in Sonnet 138. In such a context one might reword Freud's observation that civilization is founded on neuroses, to state that the best in society and the family is preserved by sexual hypocrisy. Certainly the frankness of an Othello, or of Claudio in *Much Ado,* proves Luciana's point by producing nothing but tragedy. Candor in love is so pernicious, not because truth is itself bad, but because our knowledge of it is relative, never absolute. "Being sincere," "telling it like it is" do not correspond to telling the ultimate truth; they still merely mean telling what we ourselves see as the truth (or more likely, what we want the truth to be). What one sees under the influence of sexual desire is usually totally different from what others see uninfluenced by such sentiment. Luciana is not advocating fraud by her advice to Antipholus; she is urging him merely to minimize the bitterness in the inevitable conflict of views between intimates. She has already given exactly the same advice to the resentful wife as she now gives to the erring husband: be temperate, don't force issues. The historical Ephesian magistrate, confronted by the elusive problem of St. Paul's detractors, urged the same course: "be calm and do nothing."

Circumstances justify Luciana's Machiavellian vision of sexual relations. A Desdemona or a Cordelia in the play would have made it a tragedy for sure by insisting on absolute rectitude of behavior in everyone. Adriana verges on this injudicious explicitness: "I cannot, nor I will not, hold me still" (IV. ii. 17); but fortunately even she has an involuntary inclination toward Luciana's skeptical tolerance: "Ah but I think him better than I say, . . . My heart prays for him, though my tongue do curse" (IV. ii. 25, 28). Even so Adriana's behavior illustrates the bad results of excessive concern for an ideal rapport with one's husband. Questioned by the abbess who gives sanctuary to the escaped "lunatic" that Adriana has made of her husband, Adriana admits to having persecuted him for failing to live up to her expectations:

> In bed he slept not for my urging it;
> At board he fed not for my urging it;
> Alone, it was the subject of my theme;
> In company I often glanced it;
> Still did I tell him it was vile and bad. (V. i. 63–67)

It is this same kind of nagging, about overseverity in dismissing his lieutenant Cassio, which provokes the first hint of a division of Othello from Desdemona:

> I will deny thee nothing:
> Whereon, I do beseech thee, grant me this,
> To leave me but a little to myself   (III. iii. 83–85)

Adriana also illustrates plausibly how a "good" woman may come
to treat her husband disgracefully without falling into the sadistic
misanthropy which Strindberg evokes so horridly in *The Father*.
Nevertheless, her actions are almost identical with the later wife's
excessive persecution of her husband. Adriana asserts to the abbess
that she is coming

> To fetch my poor distracted husband hence.
> Let us come in, that we may bind him fast
> And bear him home for his recovery. . . .
> This week he hath been heavy, sour, sad,
> And much different from the man he was;
> But till this afternoon his passion
> Ne'er brake into extremity of rage.
>
>   (V. i. 39–41, 45–48)

This is the kind of public disaster to which idealists can reduce
their spouses: plausibly seeking to have them consigned to restraint
as lunatics. The wife of Strindberg's captain uses a straightjacket
in the modern Swedish play.

Luciana's response to erratic behavior is obviously an infi-
nitely preferable alternative. Confronted with a brother-in-law who
is an apparent sexual maniac, she remains calm and even senses
the unrecognizable reason behind his seemingly crazy advances,
noting that they are framed "with words that in an honest suit
might move" (IV. ii. 14). Among all these sexual confusions she
refuses to get hysterical; love is synonymous with trust, and one
should be charitable to one's intimates. The real husband of
Adriana also at first remains calm when Adriana locks him out,
and he follows a friend's counsel against breaking down the
locked door of his house:

> Have patience, sir; O, let it not be so!
> Herein you war against your reputation

And draw within the compass of suspect
The unviolated honour of your wife.
Once this,—your long experience of her wisdom,
Her sober virtue, years and modesty,
Plead on her part some cause to you unknown;
And doubt not, sir, but she will well excuse
Why at this time the doors are made against you.
Be ruled by me: depart in patience,
And let us to the Tiger all to dinner,
And about evening come yourself alone
To know the reason of this strange restraint.

(III. i. 85–97)

The logic of this position is unassailable. Trust those you truly love. However, life is so unpredictable that trust is bound to be perpetually threatened. Love is thus at bottom both less and more than trust; it is the conscious suppression of plausible suspicion. Your wife may indeed actually be entertaining another man in your place. Even if this should be a fact, you would do best not to make a fuss about it, not even to insist on an explanation: "Love's best habit is in seeming trust" (Sonnet 138). We can never hope to be completely assured in sexual relationships because appearances are so deceptive. A worldly-wise Othello would have *expected* to be baffled by his wife's behavior about Cassio, and instead of killing her would have hoped at best to hear in due course of "some cause to him unknown" which would have resolved his suspicion happily.

Accepting this view leaves one with very little moral leverage as an injured party in love or marriage. It makes one more Catholic than the pope about the inappropriateness of divorce. It amounts to anticipating trouble from the start and refusing to respond negatively to it when it arrives. The attitude presupposes acceptance of apparently bad behavior in one's beloved and even one's own responsibility for causing it, because one can never fully know all the facts of another's state of mind. Adultery thus becomes only a potentially ominous symptom, not a basic issue in marriage. A mistress or a wife becomes someone you love not because of her virtue but in spite of her faults. The mark of a disintegrating relationship is not that either partner behaves badly but that this misbehavior is *held* to be significant by one of the lovers. "Grounds for divorce" are irrelevant in themselves; their mere acceptance as such means that a divorce has already occurred: someone has lost the power to love (that is, to forgive, or better still, ignore).

The Comedy of Errors is important because it shows how false plausible moral responses usually are in sexual relations. The fact that the play's specific plot is wildly implausible by traditional standards of fiction is quite unimportant; our newspapers daily describe events just as wild. That no one in the body of the play can guess the reason for all the difficulties is also true to our own everyday experience of misunderstood motives. The most significant consideration of all is that some of the "best" characters in the play make the inevitable difficulties of life even more dangerous, while others who are more skeptical minimize their dangers. Luciana suffers least and does least harm. In treating the Battle of the Sexes, Shakespeare anticipates Thurber's wry insights, but he often handles them more constructively. Luciana gets her man and seems more likely to keep him than Adriana hers, if she can also manage to educate him adequately. What should be the correct rearing and discipline of such intended husbands? Shakespeare's answer in *Love's Labour's Lost* is very radical.

<h2 style="text-align:center">"LOVE'S LABOUR'S LOST":
INTELLECTUAL LOVERS DERIDED</h2>

Novelists and poets are notorious university dropouts. Their resentment of formal education has existed for a long time. Milton's denunciation of his years at Cambridge in *Of Education* sounds like an extract from an SDS pamphlet, and his attack on the perversity of Oxford and Cambridge training may help to explain why the university wits of Shakespeare's time who sank into professional writing after successfully graduating a few years earlier made such a hash of their careers. The most pathetic example is probably Robert Greene, who died in abject poverty cursing the dramatic success of a more flexible, non-university man whose professional knowledge of the theater proved more aesthetically significant than Greene's own orthodox academic training. Greene warned his fellow graduates against this "puppet" and "Jack-of-all-trades," abusing him as a mere provincial plagiarist: "an upstart crow, beautified with our feathers." This contemptible fellow was William Shakespeare. And for all that Shakespeare could beat Greene at his own specialty of witty comedy, it seems that the criticism was mutual if we are to judge from Shakespeare's caricature of university life in *Love's Labour's Lost*. There the pretentiousness and absolutism of ambitious young intellectuals are shown to unfit them for successful performance of any demanding social role—as dramatists, as diplomats, and even as lovers.

The play opens by ridiculing the ambitions which drive young men to abandon the school of experience for years of academic abstraction (a withdrawal from the immediate realities of life about which young Americans now incline to share Shakespeare's suspicion). The King of Navarre sounds an ominous note in praise of Academia at the very start:

> Let fame, that all hunt after in their lives,
> Live register'd upon our brazen tombs
> And then grace us in the disgrace of death . . .
> And make us heirs of all eternity.
> Therefore, brave conquerors,—for so you are,
> That war against your own affections
> And the huge army of the world's desires,—
> Our late edict shall strongly stand in force:
> Navarre shall be the wonder of the world;
> Our court shall be a little Academe,
> Still and contemplative in living art.   (I. i. 1–3, 8–15)

The king's purpose sounds rather funereal, and it unnecessarily
opposes elegance and intelligence to life and emotion, rejecting the
norms of society and the public will; it is not unlike the posture of
many great American universities, in fact. The members of the
court of Navarre will live off the state of Navarre without con-
tributing to its prosperity, a relationship comparable to that accepted by some American academics. "America," they have said to
me, "is rich enough to support a few parasites like ourselves who
do nothing useful to anybody." Such a view finds one prototype in
Shakespeare's King Ferdinand. He chooses as his instructor a
virtuoso linguist as complex in his mode of expression as the most
esoteric stylists of Shakespeare's time (like John Lyly, whose
Euphues is so mannered as to draw much Shakespearean satire):

> This child of fancy that Armado hight
>   For interim to our studies shall relate
> In high-born words the worth of many a knight
>   From tawny Spain lost in the world's debate.
> How you delight, my lords, I know not, I;
> But, I protest, I love to hear him lie.   (I. i. 171–176)

That this superficially sophisticated approach has serious
limitations appears in the intolerance with which it is frequently
associated, as in King Ferdinand's treatment of one of his own
rustic retainers, Costard, who is caught by the supercilious Don
Armado in an "obscene and preposterous event" with a country
wench, Jaquenetta. Costard is regarded as criminal for being interested in the realities of sex instead of embracing the supposedly
more seductive charms of Rhetoric. Longaville, another of the erratic intellectuals at the court of Navarre, shows the same ideological ruthlessness in drafting the penalty for any tempting female
intruders into the higher realms of the Academy: they are to have
their tongues torn out. It is obviously fortunate that Costard is not
left as the only spokesman for a more natural view of life. Nature's
claims are better presented through the sardonic role of Biron, who
shares his author's considerable intellectual expertise yet devotes

much of it to the ridicule of self-sufficient intellectualism: "How well he's read, to reason against reading!" exclaims the king rue-fully (I. i. 94). Biron's suspicion of mere learning does not depend on intellectual incompetence; he *can* do what he questions in others, but wonders nevertheless if it is worth doing. His good sense boggles at the medieval asceticism of Longaville when he says: "The mind shall banquet, though the body pine" (I. i. 25). By contrast Biron asserts rather that "the end of study" is to satisfy *all* man's needs efficiently, a goal scarcely to be perfected by taking an ascetic oath:

> Come on, then; I will swear to study so,
> To know the thing I am forbid to know:
> As thus,—to study where I well may dine,
>   When I to feast expressly am forbid;
> Or study where to meet some mistress fine,
>   When mistresses from common sense are hid;
> Or, having sworn too hard a keeping oath,
> Study to break it and not break my troth.
>
> (I. i. 59–66)

This hearty skepticism comes close to that of the mature sonnets: the function of intellect is not to exalt man but to avert inconvenience and disaster. By comparison, the ecstatic view of reason expounded by Socrates in Plato's dialogues seems merely hallucinatory to Biron, particularly in its more bookish modern forms:

> Why, all delights are vain; but that most vain,
> Which with pain purchased doth inherit pain:
> As, painfully to pore upon a book
>   To seek the light of truth; while truth the while
> Doth falsely blind the eyesight of his look:
>   Light seeking light doth light of light beguile: . . .
> Small have continual plodders ever won
>   Save base authority from others' books. . . .
> Too much to know is to know nought but fame.
>
> (I. i. 72–77, 86–87, 92)

Biron's advice is similar to the confident advice of the opening sonnets of the cycle, which counsel talented youth to pursue practical
wisdom and action rather than be aloofly complacent. This affected
air of jaded authority gives Biron more than a hint of smugness
presaging a painful process of self-discovery comparable to that in
the *Sonnets:*

> I believe, although I seem so loath,
> I am the last that will last keep his oath.
>
> (I. i. 160–161)

Essentially, his starting position is that the man who understands
human limitations will allow for them in his calculations and be
at least less likely than the idealist to fail in maintaining his obligations. The skeptic is likely to be the only trustworthy man.

Biron at once illustrates his prescience by showing his friends
that their vow to avoid women cannot be maintained even for a
single day because of the impending arrival of the charming daughter of the King of France with her court, on a diplomatic mission.
King Ferdinand admits that necessity requires the temporary
suspension of their oath, and Biron observes that

> Necessity will make us all forsworn
> Three thousand times within this three years' space; . . .
> If I break faith, this word shall speak for me;
> I am forsworn on 'mere necessity.'   (I. i. 150–151, 154–155)

Human nature must necessarily take its own failure as axiomatic,
no matter what sophistries may be employed in exculpation. Biron
at least may handle his inevitable embarrassments more creatively
than the rest because he expects them and can prepare his defenses
in advance:

> I'll lay my head to any good man's hat,
> These oaths and laws will prove an idle scorn.
>
> (I. i. 310–311)

Of course, the play's plot vindicates these anticipations, and one is left to observe that in contrast to Biron a naive young idealist like Longaville proves throughout to be a most sinister figure. It is he who is most convinced that "the mind shall banquet, though the body pine." According to modern psychology Longaville, as the most repressed personality, is also likely to be the most dangerous one, and it is indeed this keenest of the intended recluses who favors tearing out the tongue of any woman who braves their ban on female company. Moreover, when his suppressed sexuality finally drives him to reject the discipline which he has earlier favored, Longaville's rationalization of his dishonesty depends on cheap sophistries:

> Did not the heavenly rhetoric of thine eye,
>   'Gainst whom the world cannot hold argument,
> Persuade my heart to this false perjury?
> Vows for thee broke deserve not punishment.
> A woman I forswore; but I will prove,
>   Thou being a goddess, I forswore not thee:
> My vow was earthly, thou a heavenly love;
>   Thy grace being gain'd cures all disgrace in me.
>   (IV. iii. 60–67)

The argument comes down to saying to the lady in the case that the intensity of feeling she generates in her lover justifies him in disregarding the oath of celibacy which Longaville imposed on himself: he vowed not to indulge in earthly passion, but this is a heavenly one and therefore not covered by vows of mere sexual abstinence. Any woman who is in the least perceptive will be suspicious of such facile flattery: pseudo-mysticism is not an adequate disguise for dishonesty. Evidently Longaville is now reduced to the same level as Biron at the start of the play when he promised that he would, "having sworn too hard a keeping oath, / Study to break it."

In contrast, Biron's rationalization of the gallants' fickleness is at least consistent with his initial position that learning divorced from social relationships and worldly satisfactions is not true learning at all. Essentially he develops the argument presented by Socrates in Plato's *Symposium*, that the sexual urge will provide the best initial incentives for the discovery of universal beauty by making one aware of it in specific cases in those around us. Biron thus argues that love of women is a necessary part of successful scholarship, since the attainment of sexual communion proves to be both a catalyst of awareness and its ultimate field of study:

> love, first learned in a lady's eyes,
> Lives not alone immured in the brain;
> But, with the motion of all elements,
> Courses as swift as thought in every power,
> And gives to every power a double power,
> Above their functions and their offices....
> From women's eyes this doctrine I derive:
> They sparkle still the right Promethean fire;
> They are the books, the arts, the academes,
> That show, contain and nourish all the world:
> Else none at all in aught proves excellent.
>
> (IV. iii. 327–332, 350–354)

Biron makes lively use of Platonic theories about the advantages of sexual reinforcements for study, without assenting to the ultimate Platonic rejection of sex in favor of intellectual sublimation. This pragmatism is a striking example of Shakespeare's characteristic exclusion of transcendental values from his plays; the same down-to-earth inclination causes Shakespeare to model the male roles of this comedy nominally on historical figures borrowed from oddments of French history rather than on the archetypes of contemporary Italianate comedy, with its facile sentimentality.

The idea that Shakespeare is in revolt against contemporary displays of mere literary virtuosity and learning is more compatible with Biron's own wit and intellectual expertise than might at first appear. It is true that Biron merely seems to affect the role of rebel and heretic in seeking "to know the thing I am forbid to know"

(I. i. 60) and in defending "barbarism." What he often does is to justify the demands of common sense without surrendering the charms of high style. This makes him both a wit and a realist, unlike his friends. Essentially he finds smart and picturesque reasons for simply doing what is natural; and because he is always in touch with the world of food and drink and sex, his ingenious advocacy of female companionship is no sentimental philosophizing but a conscious rationalization of the necessity for women in any humane society.

One of the most striking things about Shakespeare is this respect for women's social role; for him they are above all the conscious sustainers of society and culture, as are modern American women. Shakespeare's comic heroines are extraordinarily proficient socially and sexually: they are the arbiters of social relations, deeply in harmony with the biological needs of the race. This does not mean that for Shakespeare they are men's absolute superiors, merely that in matters of emotion and human relationships their sensibility almost invariably determines the outcome. The prime sources of disaster in Shakespeare's plays are to be found in women who neurotically forget their biological role (like Lady Macbeth) or their social tact (like Desdemona and Cordelia), or who attempt to seize physical supremacy from the male (like Queen Margaret or Cleopatra). By contrast, the comedies are governed by women whose commitment to sexual intercourse and childbearing extends to the extravagant achievements of Helena in *All's Well,* who weds and beds Bertram and bears his children against his will and largely without his knowledge, reducing him to a state of almost abject submission. It is not surprising that Shaw saw in her a prototype of his "new woman," comparable to his other model, the St. Joan of *Henry VI.* (He also wrote a playlet about the Dark Lady of the *Sonnets.*)

The ladies in *Love's Labour's Lost* are no exception to this conception of women. The mere arrival of the French princess demonstrates the impracticality of the king's misogynic seclusion, and she does not hesitate to stress the self-destructiveness of his commitment openly:

> I hear your grace hath sworn out house-keeping:
> 'Tis deadly sin to keep that oath, my lord,
> And sin to break it.   (II. i. 104–106)

The contrast between the ladies' open-air lodging and the intended monastic seclusion of the young men during their three-year academic project is intended to stress the difference between university book-learning and natural wisdom. The visiting princess and her ladies are appropriately lodged in tents in the midst of the countryside, for they freely accept natural urges and activities. The princess hunts the deer boldly, and her ladies share that frank recognition of sexual desire which cost Costard some censure before their arrival. Costard's hearty obscenities about the mechanics of cuckoldry are cheerfully matched by Maria, and Boyet's by Rosaline (IV. i. 122 ff.); like fashionable modern American women, Shakespeare's young women feel no nervousness about participating in such bawdy repartees with men. Among themselves the ladies are also prompt to sexual innuendos (V. ii. 13 ff.). By contrast the studious young lords are invariably prudes—even Biron never extends his vivacity and skepticism to bawdiness. The pompous prosecution and judgment of Costard's misconduct with Jaquenetta typify the stiff solemnity to which love of academic discipline and learning encourages the young men.

The worldly wisdom of Biron at least comes nearer to the author's own attitude than does that of the other young aristocrats; he resembles the speaker in the *Sonnets* who is invested with the full verbal range and intellectual virtuosity of which Shakespeare is capable. These literary gifts certainly rival the rhetorical skills which authors like Lyly, Greene, and Marlowe perfected during their education at Cambridge. Biron's vivacious personality is surprisingly close to Jonson's sketch of Shakespeare's own, in *Discoveries:* "He was, indeed, honest, and of an open and free nature;

had an excellent phantasy, brave notions, and gentle expressions, wherein he flowed with that facility that sometimes it was necessary he should be stopped." It is curious to see how Biron's career duplicates this pattern; he suffers exactly the check which Jonson clearly sought to impose on Shakespeare. And like the speaker in the *Sonnets,* Biron also meets his defeat at the hand of a Dark Lady, the brunette Rosaline. It is useful to note the play's final judgment on the author's own mastery of language with which he so largely endows Biron.

As we have seen, from the start Biron's suppleness of mind far surpasses the stilted academic thinking of his friends. Rosaline's testimony is partial but nevertheless appropriate, for she sees in him the tact and discrimination largely lacking in his friends:

> a merrier man,
> Within the limit of becoming mirth,
> I never spent an hour's talk withal:
> His eye begets occasion for his wit;
> For every object that the one doth catch
> The other turns to a mirth-moving jest,
> Which his fair tongue, conceit's expositor,
> Delivers in such apt and gracious words
> That aged ears play truant at his tales
> And younger hearings are quite ravished;
> So sweet and voluble is his discourse.   (II. i. 66–76)

Yet Biron's lively sense of his own virtues betrays him into a kind of hubris:

> And though I have for barbarism spoke more
> Than for that angel knowledge you can say,
> Yet confident I'll keep what I have swore
> And bide the penance of each three years' day.
>   (I. i. 112–115)

Given his greater realism, it does seem plausible that he should undertake the project with better chances of success than his col-

leagues; but Shakespeare carefully arranges that the play's most
gifted character shall suffer the same humiliations that befall all the
male characters, whether from pretentiousness like Don Armado or
Holofernes in the pageant, or from mishandled sexual susceptibility like the other lords and even Costard. Often these failures are
duplicated in several characters' misfortunes, and they extend
even to such minor male roles as that of the forester who awkwardly tries to turn a compliment to the princess (IV. i. 9 ff.), or
the poor parson trying to rival his more sophisticated companions
in the pageant.

But Biron's downfall is the more significant because he is so
clearly superior to the rest in awareness. His worst failing is not
misuse of wit and subtlety but lack of consistency: he cannot always
bring to his own love that witty detachment he brings sardonically
to bear on the affairs of others. His involuntary loss of poise is
drastically illustrated in his first exchange with Rosaline, in which
his heavy courtesies are smartly rejected by the lady, whose feelings are more under control. Just as the shallower Boyet finds her
"too hard for me" (II. i. 261), so Biron loses poise and falls into
mere reproaches: "You must not be so quick" (II. i. 118). While
no flatulent Don Armado, Biron as a lover illustrates a more
sophisticated form of the same defect the flamboyant Spaniard
shows when his linguistic finesse is grossly irrelevant to his experience. This lapse in Biron is what Margaret and Boyet combine to
attack: "Not a word with him but a jest." —"And every jest but
a word" (II. i. 215). By the end of Act III, Biron frankly recognizes that he has been reduced to the level of Costard by the force
of sexual instincts for which even he did not adequately allow. The
result is a complex state of mind surprisingly close to that of
Sonnet 130:

> What? I love! I sue! I seek a wife!
> A woman, that is like a German clock,
> Still a-repairing, ever out of frame,
> And never going aright, being a watch,

But being watch'd that it may still go right!
Nay, to be perjured, which is worst of all;
And, among three, to love the worst of all;
A whitely wanton with a velvet brow,
With two pitch-balls stuck in her face for eyes;
Ay, and by heaven, one that will do the deed
Though Argus were her eunuch and her guard:
And I to sigh for her! to watch for her!
To pray for her! Go to; it is a plague
That Cupid will impose for my neglect
Of his almighty dreadful little might.
Well, I will love, write, sigh, pray, sue, groan:
Some men must love my lady and some Joan.

(III. i. 191–207)

Like the speaker in Sonnet 130, Biron now has no illusions
about himself or even his mistress—if anything, he thinks of her as
worse than she appears to us in the play. He has also none of
Longaville's mystical fantasies about the heavenliness of the emotions which he feels. His approach is stoic rather than tragic, but
even as he accepts the inevitability of sexual love, it still appears
to him as much a monstrosity and an intellectual aberration as it
did to Euripides' Phaedra. Like Euripides' chorus, he regards all
lovers as largely victims, not initiators, of their desire, and as being
doomed by the dictates of a divinity whose will crushes the initiative of its human instruments. All that is left to them is a rueful
acceptance of their fate, to be made as gracefully and honorably as
occasion permits.

Even this course has little appeal for Biron: alone of the
young apostates he does not confidently welcome their recovered
sexual freedom. He himself had gloated over his companions'
downfall while he still was able to conserve at least the appearance
of integrity:

I, that am honest; I, that hold it sin
To break the vow I am engaged in;
I am betray'd, by keeping company

> With men like men of inconstancy.
> When shall you see me write a thing in rhyme?
> Or groan for love?   (IV. iii. 177–182)

Once again the hubristic note is heard for a moment, but Biron's own comic downfall instantly follows with his friends' discovery of one of his love letters, so that he also is forced to exclaim: "Guilty, my lord, guilty! I confess, I confess" (IV. iii. 206). Thereafter, recognizing how he has delighted in his own hypocritical sarcasms at his friends' expense, he readily foresees just what kind of tangles the young women will involve them in, if these ladies know of their emotional advantage. While the ever simple-minded Longaville innocently proposes: "Now to plain-dealing," Biron drily warns: "be first advised, / In conflict that you get the sun of them" because "Light wenches may prove plagues to men forsworn" (IV. iii. 385).

The enormous last scene of the play (around a thousand lines in length) is an elaborate exposition and analysis of the whole cycle of sexual courtship once young men are committed wholeheartedly to it. Far from being merely a clever display of rhetorical and dramatic pyrotechnics, the scene is a systematic commentary on the difficulties of the deployment and communication of emotion between the sexes. Neither the aristocrats' Masque of the Russians nor the professional men's Pageant of the Nine Worthies is merely an exercise in parody of contemporary literary modes; both illustrate classic emotional responses to testing situations. The apprehensive young aristocrats are too unsure of themselves to approach their young women frankly; they are still uncertain how far they dare avow their affection and are also unwilling to admit their grotesque deficiencies in trustworthiness. To distract attention from their limitations they deliberately affect false personalities as erratic "Russians," supposedly exotic and fascinating roles but actually personae so artificial and alien to their own natures that they are betrayed into disastrous incoherence and confusions of identity. As a consequence of this overcleverness all, both male and female, cease to be what they seem: the young men pretend to be romantic foreigners, and in revenge the masked Rosaline pretends she is the princess, and so on. Perhaps nothing proves more humiliating to the supposedly dashing young suitors than for each to find that in his nervous masquerade he has proposed to the wrong mistress; so unstable is such a pretentious lover's outlook that he not only loses the sense of his own identity but is incapable even of recognizing the woman who has supposedly entranced him. There is a total lack of true mutuality and awareness in such mannered courtships. The young men are too ambitious to be either good students or good lovers.

As usual it is Biron who sees that the only hope for lovers as pretentiously incompetent as they have proved lies in the painstaking and painful construction of a more realistic relationship with their women, founded on a humble, even humiliating openness on the part of the lover, in which he consciously admits his limitations while hoping to win the understanding of his beloved, instead of trying to fascinate her by his supposed wit and by romantic appeals to her imagination. Distinction is impossible for the victim of sexual desire because sexual desire is necessarily a defeat of his self-sufficiency and often destroys his powers of intellectual discrimination. Instead of seeking to capture his lady by satisfying her supposed desires for a virtuoso lover, Biron now appeals to Rosaline's mercifulness by accepting what almost begins to sound like a Christian martyrdom by her wit:

> Thus pour the stars down plagues for perjury.
>   Can any face of brass hold longer out?
> Here stand I: lady, dart thy skill at me;
>   Bruise me with scorn, confound me with a flout;
> Thrust thy sharp wit quite through my ignorance;
>   Cut me to pieces with thy keen conceit; . . .
> Taffeta phrases, silken terms precise,
>   Three-piled hyperboles, spruce affectation,
> Figures pedantical; these summer-flies
>   Have blown me full of maggot ostentation:

> I do forswear them; and I here protest, ...
> Henceforth my wooing mind shall be express'd
> In russet yeas and honest kersey noes.
>   (V. ii. 394–399, 406–410, 412–413)

Thus Shakespeare brings his hero to the same wry conclusions as the gifted protagonist of his sonnets. Biron is forced to admit that he has not even the wit to court "a whitely wanton" effectively. And in so doing Biron as a lover has to surrender reliance on the appeal of that brilliance of style which makes this early Shakespearean play such a striking example of Elizabethan poetic exuberance.

Each of the other major male characters in *Love's Labour's Lost* initially displays a classic variant of Elizabethan verbal extravagance, be it Don Armado's explicit Euphuism or Holofernes' humanistic pedantry or Longaville's Platonic absolutism. And all suffer a therapeutic catharsis like Biron's, through a public humiliation occasioned by their misapplication of these skills. The aristocrats' initial desire to be practiced scholars destroys their good sense and thereby their amatory hopes; the professional scholars' ambition to cast themselves as the heroes of the antique world they have laboriously studied makes them even more ridiculous. Their literary pageant aspires to present the pedants as heroes like Hercules and Alexander; but though these "heroes" receive no heroic challenge, the mere jests of the courtiers in the audience are enough to shatter their composure. The pedant Holofernes ruefully admits the final defeat of the professor: "You have put me out of countenance" (V. ii. 624). After his complacent "hectoring" of his fellow scholars whenever they make trivial mistakes of phrasing or decorum, this almost equals the humiliation of Biron's recognition that he cannot manipulate his own feelings as well as he can twist words and ideas.

But having been forced to accept the harsh truth that he is no hero, Holofernes finds the continued raillery of his supercilious audience not merely offensive but vicious. His reproach to the jeer-

ing aristocrats ultimately rings louder and truer than all their
jibes: "This is not generous, not gentle, not humble" (V. ii. 632).
With similar good sense Costard has already defended the pathetic
curate who lost his nerve as he injudiciously tried to portray Alexander: "There, an't shall please you: a foolish mild man; an honest
man, look you, and soon dashed. He is a marvellous good neigh-
bour, faith" (V. ii. 586-587). It is left for the extravagant Spaniard
Don Armado to rise highest above his own conventional identity
and to speak with timeless compassion and candor in defense of the
spirit of Hector, whom the wits have ungraciously ridiculed: "The
sweet war-man is dead and rotten; sweet chucks, beat not the bones
of the buried: when he breathed, he was a man" (V. ii. 666–668).
Once again in the play, smart wits are unequal to the challenge of
serious emotion: their male victims' identities prove as unpredictable as those of their mistresses.

Thus the aristocrats as a group undergo a climactic humiliation at the hands of their supposedly ridiculous victims. And for
the king, who launched their whole unwise course of action in
pursuit of academic distinction, an even worse misfortune is re-
served. The courtiers' failure to handle tactfully the bitter reality of
death and defeat for which Don Armado has just become the unexpected spokesman finally hurts even the most poised and sensible
character in the play. The French princess learns of the death of her
father, and instead of consoling her the king's flowery rhetoric
merely upsets her further: "I understand you not: my griefs are
double" (V. ii. 762). Thus the king once more discovers that he
cannot cope tactfully with serious issues: his abstract idealism and
mechanical finesse are irrelevant to the basic matters of human
emotion, love and death. It is left to Biron to interpret the king's
feelings, knowing as Biron now does that "Honest plain words
best pierce the ear of grief" (V. ii. 763). With this clue to the
young men's real concern, the ladies at last begin to take their
lovers more seriously, but still not sentimentally. The harsh pen-
ances laid upon each suitor are less punishments for previous shal-

lowness and flippancy than disciplines to test the new sobriety of
their intentions. They are set to study in a new school, that of real
deprival and suffering. Rosaline requires of Biron that

> You shall this twelvemonth term from day to day
> Visit the speechless sick and still converse
> . With groaning wretches; and your task shall be,
> With all the fierce endeavour of your wit
> To enforce the pained impotent to smile.

(V. ii. 860–864)

Thus is a lover's egocentric wit to be tempered by reality. As
the author, Shakespeare himself clearly needs none of Jonson's
admonitions against misuse of his own verbal fluency: in Biron he
has vicariously submitted his poetic gifts to the bitter discipline of
experience. But we should recognize that Shakespeare's point
about the dangerous conflict between wit and desire has been made
again and again throughout the play for his audience as much as
for his characters. The play is made up of a series of situations in
which failure occurs because intellectual achievement has been
made a sufficient goal. Wit divorced from immediate experience is
inimical to all the finer emotions: the king treats Costard contemptuously, Longaville threatens women with mutilation, and
Biron finds that his finely penned speeches merely lead to ridicule
by the skeptical ladies. The play ends where most amatory comedy
begins, with a minimal recognition that love may be possible between the ladies and their admirers. All the usual resources of a
talented lover are shown by the ladies to be pretentious subterfuges
used by timorous lovers to conceal their own dishonorable identities. Even Biron's formal rejection of rhetoric is deftly punctured
when Rosaline shows that it is itself a clever rhetorical performance
(V. ii. 416).

I wonder that more scholars are not surprised by the failure
of rhetoric to achieve a conventional happy ending for the play.
The ladies are not brought by mere verbal skill to accept their

lovers. Shakespeare clearly intends this rejection of the lovers by the women (including Jaquenetta!) as a rejection on his own part of the idea that conventional modes of courtship can lead to successful marriage. The untempered excellences of youth are made to seem unfit for the demands of such a strenuous relationship. Indeed no truly discriminating Shakespearean comic heroine is naive enough to risk surrender to the bookish courtliness that helps to bring about Juliet's ruin by encouraging her to make the kind of premature marriage which later earns Helena a comparably obtuse husband (as the next chapter shows). Marriage is too complex and demanding a relationship to be undertaken by sexual amateurs: the correct initiation is not the exchange of sentimental flatteries, but tough social work with the sick and dying.

Many young Americans are now beginning to feel that they are not up to the demands of marriage but only to those of temporary liaisons. They are beginning to understand that a successful marriage makes very severe demands on traditional female psychology, particularly if the young man is an intellectual. It was to Shakespeare's advantage that the roles in his comedies which provide prototypes for modern emancipated young women were performed by boy actors, who could bring to the parts a firmness of manner and an incisiveness of mind that young women were then only recently and very unevenly beginning to acquire under the impetus of humanistic education. Even today it is extremely hard for a young woman not to surrender to instinct and take as a significant partner the first acceptable male who presents himself. If he is an intellectual, this kind of premature commitment carries the further financial penalty that she will very likely have to support him through college, delaying the family she wants while enduring the pretensions of an inexperienced spouse.

If we apply the argument of *Love's Labour's Lost* to our own times, it looks as if all young men should be removed for a while from any intellectual environment as soon as they are graduated from high school. Something like this is advocated by authorities as different as Maria Montessori, S. I. Hayakawa, and Mao Tse-tung. The aim is to separate young men from tempting marriage part-ners, whom at present they tend to debauch intellectually, emo-tionally, and physically, because they have so little sense of the range and nature of human relationships; probably marriage at any age under twenty-five should also be systematically discour-aged everywhere, as in China at present. Moreover, by working in the Peace Corps, or even in the armed services, young men would discover how the majority of men actually live, feel, and suffer. One has only to read the program for SDS industrial penetration to understand that young men's total ignorance of workers' experi-ence is closely comparable to their naive idea that true sexuality is merely free sexual intercourse.

Women of some sophistication claim that they can quickly identify those who have completed military service or a long stint in government or business before becoming professional intellec-tuals. These men are supposedly less likely to marry sentimental students, more gifted with illuminating insights than expert in scholarship, and more likely to work for solid accomplishments than for those fantasy solutions to the world's ills which frequently result in mass violence and worse confusions than those that pro-voked them. One possible reason for the intellectuals' hatred of the professional businessman or successful politician may lie in the intellectuals' sense of their own comparative ineffectiveness in the practical world, an ineffectiveness that verges on becoming a proof of virtue. The university cults of Stevenson and McCarthy confirm that American intellectuals love a sophisticated loser; like Oxford, American universities are "the home of lost causes." And this spirit even enters their own disciplines: a professor who has writ-ten a best-seller is held by his diffident colleagues to have betrayed the truth out of a mercenary or ostentatious spirit.

Put at their crudest, these views suggest that too many Ameri-can intellectuals are frightened by success; to them failure seems less oppressive and far more picturesque. Herzog is their ideal, and

Willie Loman what they make of everyone else. The weak personality finds it safer to contemplate passive tragedy than heroic failure or vigorous comedy and prefers sentimental or abortive love affairs to sustained marital relationships. It is no coincidence that in *Love and Death in the American Novel* Leslie Fiedler has already suggested that American novelists resemble the young men in *Love's Labour's Lost* (one of Shakespeare's earliest plays) in being unable to handle a mature sexual relationship. That Shakespeare's later plays portray figures who do succeed in this is one reason why he is so essential an author in the American literary pantheon. Without him there would be few examples of successful love available to American readers. However, I hope by the end of this book to show that Fiedler's judgment is partial, in that at least one modern American play, Albee's *Virginia Woolf,* succeeds brilliantly in the Shakespearean vein, by deliberately exceeding the limits of immature infatuations. But first we need to see how Shakespeare would offset the female variants of the neurotic threats to sexuality mapped out in *Love's Labour's Lost.*

"THE TAMING OF THE SHREW"

OR

HOW A TALENTED WOMAN CAN
BECOME A SUCCESSFUL WIFE
AND BE HAPPY

Of course, there are substantial reasons for the social disabilities that women have always suffered. Nothing is more false than the propaganda of Women United for the Attainment of Universal Peace by Electing a Female President and myriads of similar groups. Without considering the contemporary examples, one can see that women in high office have historically too often made excellent competition for Nero and Caligula (who themselves owed a great deal to Agrippina, the mother of one and sister of the other). Beginning with the amazing imperialism of Semiramis in the ninth century B.C., and running through Cleopatra's aggressive pursuit of Egyptian hegemony over the eastern Mediterranean (of which more later), a remarkable number of women rulers have started trouble. In the Middle Ages, Joan of Arc does not exactly corroborate the idea that women make pacific leaders. For more modern examples one might examine Catherine de' Medici's involvement in the St. Bartholomew's Day Massacre, the vagaries of Catherine the Great, and those of the last major Manchu, Dowager Empress Tz'u Hsi, who started the Boxer Rebellion. The sinister Lady Macbeth is Shakespeare's representation of the dangers of such domineering women. The best one can say of more successful women rulers, like Elizabeth and Maria Theresa, is that they killed no more people than most male rulers, while exacting rather more servile flattery and tyrannizing over their courtiers with some pretty perverse whims.

The gifted woman of less exalted rank finds that sentimental sexuality often places her at a social disadvantage. Clever men want impassive women on whom to project their fantasies, but female administrators and intellectuals are not always able or willing to pretend to be stock figures forever immobilized in picturesque poses. Rejecting sentiment, and often the complicating demands of family life too, many gifted women find in professionalism a compensatory way of living that only the most egotistical men can endure. The unmarried professional woman is thus by nature prone to react against the traditional "feminine" virtues that encourage personal relations, and tends to enforce a rigorous formal discipline on her colleagues. Many distinguished women in the academic profession are far more exacting than a top sergeant at his most overpowering. Their extraordinary precision of thought and mastery of particulars make them close to impregnable intellectually and emotionally. As *Love's Labour's Lost* shows, nothing is more salutary to a gifted mind than a little humiliation or sub-ordination by its superiors, its equals, or even its inferiors. But to professional women such treatment must always seem (as it too often actually is) mere contempt for their sex or automatic dis-crimination. Thus women in authority are all too often relentless to others in their profession, yet savagely intolerant of criticism of their own performance by anyone else.

But such a situation is neither normal nor inevitable. It is a testimony to Shakespeare's profound respect for women that, like Milton, he regards them as more capable than men of the finest social discriminations and that he devotes as much time in his plays to the problem of the maturation of the gifted woman as to that of the brilliant male. Most of his plays turn on the success or failure with which extraordinary women apply their capacities to the ad-vantage of their societies.

The particular question of what kind of sexual maturity is available to the unusually intelligent woman is most explicitly handled in another early play, *The Taming of the Shrew,* which affords a paradoxical companion piece to *Love's Labour's Lost.* The latter shows the faults to which young men are prone, above all self-defeating pretentiousness which must be cured by repeated public humiliation and by submission to mundane social responsi-bilities—a penalty which we shall see imposed so often in later Shakespearean plays as to become almost a formula. With women the potential faults are far more pathological. The young men may repress their sexuality and often become accident-prone, like Romeo or Hamlet, because of their emotional instability. But am-bitious young women are far more vulnerable to deep psychological disorders, of which Joan's transvestism and diabolism in *Henry VI* are characteristic symptoms. Even more characteristic are Lady Macbeth's prayers to be "unsexed" and Volumnia's vicarious satis-faction in virile bloodlust through her son's massacres. Neither a Macbeth nor a Coriolanus nor even a Lear can master such per-verse femininity in its advanced forms. We can only consider what

possibilities there are of arresting this kind of corruption before it is
too fully developed to cure.

In *The Taming of the Shrew* we may indeed seem to see a
labor worthy of the talents of the Hercules celebrated in the
Pageant of the Worthies, the transformation of the neurotic shrew
Katharina into the poised matron who dominates the play's conclusion. Katharina undergoes as harsh a purgation as the young
lovers in *Love's Labour's Lost,* and for very much the same reason:
she suffers from an unthinking fascination with courtship and
love, the lack of which is driving her nearly to frenzy at the start
of the play. Her sadistic persecution of her attractive younger
sister is clearly motivated by envious rage, as she confesses to her
father:

> Nay, now I see
> She is your treasure, she must have a husband;
> I must dance bare-foot on her wedding day
> And for your love to her lead apes in hell.   (II. i. 31–34)

The irony is, of course, that when her preoccupation drives her to
accept even as bizarre a suitor as Petruchio, she finds the devotions
of a husband even worse than the misfortunes of a single life. In
this play Shakespeare shows us as harsh a view of the problems of
marital accommodation as he had of the frustrating confusions of
courtship in *Love's Labour's Lost.* However, *The Taming of the
Shrew* also sustains the earlier play's sardonic view of courtship in
the underplot of Bianca's marriage. It is very interesting that this
more sentimental courtship is firmly subordinated to the harsher
theme of the battle of the sexes between Katharina and Petruchio:
Shakespeare seems to favor the English tradition of farcical realism
over the neatly plotted neoclassicism of such Italian comedies as
Ariosto's *I Suppositi* (from which the subplot material of the
Shrew is derived by way of Gascoigne's free translation, *The
Supposes* of 1566).

The grotesque incoherence of everyday life emphatically sets the key for Shakespeare's play, from its opening with the drunken entrance of the tinker Christopher Sly, whose degeneracy provides the theme for the two scenes of the Induction. Like the supposedly misogynistic farce of Katharina's "taming," whose pattern it prefigures, this curious opening to the play has been the subject of critical censure, but it is treated far more meaningfully than a superficial reading suggests. Sly's condition is judged to be hopelessly depraved:

> O monstrous beast! how like a swine he lies!
> Grim death, how foul and loathsome is thine image.
>
> (Ind., i. 34–35)

This pathological state amply justifies any shock treatment that may startle him out of acceptance of so pernicious a view of his own identity. Shakespeare shows us how feeble a sense of reality man has by plausibly transforming Sly's disintegrated personality into a confidently lordly one, which he finally accepts as his proper role. The rest of the play is a series of amplifications, above all through Katharina, of this theme of the fragility of human identity and its proneness to transmutations, for good or ill.

We pass instantly from contemplating the depraving alcoholic intoxication of Sly to the equally depraving amatory intoxication of Lucentio. Like the young lords of *Love's Labour's Lost,* Lucentio illustrates his callowness by a naive devotion to the study of philosophy at the University of Padua, which he is convinced will lead inevitably to "virtuous deeds." It is left to his servant Tranio to play the wiser role of Biron, by advising a better course of study:

> I am in all affected as yourself; . . .
> Only, good master, while we do admire
> This virtue and this moral discipline,
> Let's be no stoics nor no stocks, I pray;
> Or so devote to Aristotle's checks
> As Ovid be an outcast quite abjured:

> Balk logic with acquaintance that you have
> And practise rhetoric in your common talk; . . .
> No profit grows where is no pleasure ta'en.
>
> (I. i. 26, 29–35, 39)

Ironically, Lucentio at once takes this advice, with an absoluteness that quite discredits his academic enthusiasm of the
previous moment. Struck with sexual fascination for the passing
Bianca, he is immediately reduced to a stupor comparable to that
of Christopher Sly, much to the distress of Tranio, who perceives
the pernicious lethargy which such intoxications induce:

> Nay, then, 'tis time to stir him from his trance.
> I pray, awake, sir.   (I. i. 182–183)

Unfortunately, Lucentio declines further with farcical promptness.
He decides instantly to abandon his studies and become "a meaner
man" (I. i. 210), and goes so far as to predict his ultimate humiliating condition as Bianca's husband, in wishing to "be a slave, to
achieve that maid" (I. i. 224). His commitment to his new debased
position appears in his choice of name—Cambio—the man who has
lost his identity. He deliberately surrenders his rank and most of
his initiative to his servant Tranio.

Even in Lucentio's role as Latin tutor to Bianca, evil omens
pursue him: of all the lines of Ovid that he might choose to gloss,
he has the bad luck to fall on these, from *Heroides* (I. 33): "Here
flowed the River Simois, here is the Sigeian land; here stood the
lofty palace of Priam" (III. i. 28–29). The lines evoke the ruins of
the city of Troy, a monument to the disastrous consequences of
sexual passion and unqualified delight in female beauty. The letter
of the lonely Penelope to her straying husband from which the
lines are taken also hardly suggests that marriage is a blessed state,
when one's husband may be abroad for twenty years.

Lucentio's transformation produces even more distressing effects on his father Vincentio, who finds himself reduced to the

same bemused condition as Antipholus of Ephesus in *The Comedy of Errors*. Confronted with the substitute for his son, he fears the worst: "O he hath murdered his master!" (V. i. 90). And for his pains he is called "madman," "lunatic." Finally the police are ordered to "carry this mad knave to the gaol." The effect of this distressing situation is intensified by Vincentio's having already been subjected to a crazy encounter on the road to Padua with Petruchio and a newly flexible Katharina, who humors her husband by greeting the aged Vincentio as a "young budding virgin" (IV. v. 37). Such are the strange consequences of sexual relationships; and of course Shakespeare's wry sense of these pathological effects is totally lacking in his source, Gascoigne's version of Ariosto.

Furthermore, this distorted fashionable material from sentimental comedy serves chiefly as a foil to the central action, the bizarre relationship between Katharina and Petruchio, which satirically runs the gamut of the discords inevitable in any passionate relationship between two gifted people, such as we have already seen in the *Sonnets*. For Petruchio and Katharina are not the ludicrous stereotypes we expect in farce. Katharina in particular is a magnificent creation—a prototype for such later misanthropic heroines as Beatrice and Isabella. She illustrates all the evil potentialities of soured virtue summed up in the concluding line of Sonnet 94: "Lilies that fester smell far worse than weeds." Unlike Bianca, who affects a coy mask to conceal her egotism, Katharina's more legitimate sense of her own merits has turned her resentment at their neglect into shrewishness. There is something of the tragic obtuseness of a Hotspur or a Coriolanus in her fiery independence of convention:

> Why, sir, I trust I may have leave to speak;
> And speak I will; I am no child, no babe:
> Your betters have endured me say my mind,
> And if you cannot, best you stop your ears.
> My tongue will tell the anger of my heart,

> Or else my heart concealing it will break,
> And rather than it shall, I will be free
> Even to the uttermost, as I please, in words.

> (IV. iii. 73–80)

A modern mind instinctively sympathizes with such sincerity, and so does Shakespeare, self-destructive though he knows it
to be. This dangerous forthrightness and promptness distinguish
his most dynamic figures—Othello, Cordelia, Kent, even Lear—
but it is precisely their lack of "Machiavellian" flexibility which
dooms such characters. Katharina's virtue is that she has retained a
capacity for suppleness, even though she clearly begins the play in a
neurotic state of mind. Her beating of the bound Bianca (II. i. 21)
is obviously pathological; and even her wit has a strain of physical
violence (II. i. 220ff.) which implies a mind close to breakdown.
Thus, like Christopher Sly, her disintegrating personality seems to
justify almost any kind of shock therapy; and it is the virtue of
Petruchio to grasp that a personality of her aggressiveness necessarily possesses enormous possibilities. Petruchio brings to his unconventional choice of a wife all the mature skepticism and contempt for sentimental expectations in love which appear in the
most subtle of Shakespeare's sonnets praising the unconventional
attractions of the Dark Lady.

But unlike the sonnets, the play allows us to participate fully
in Petruchio's demonstration of the unexpected fact that the offensive defects of Katharina are signs of a worthier personality than
the sly charms of "fair Bianca." For example, during her persecution by her husband, Katharina resents not only his insensitivity to
herself but also his supposed cruelty to his servants; when he
strikes one she protests: "Patience, I pray you; 'twas a fault un-
witting" (IV. i. 159). Unfortunately, her legitimate sense of her
own superiority to almost everyone around her blinds her to the
fact that even by her own standards she is fallible. What has
alienated everyone until Petruchio appears is her failure to recognize that even the most gifted man or woman may be incapable of

handling truth with propriety. She is almost as obtuse as those whose shallowness she rightly censures; and the result of her forthrightness has only been to increase the frustrations that she resents. However, Petruchio is far from breaking her spirit in "taming" her; he does not deny her freedom of expression, but teaches her a more effective social stance. At the end of the play Katharina is if anything more dominant than ever because she has learned how to phrase her attacks irresistibly, by humbly recognizing her own limitations and thus disarming resistance. The necessary prelude to the effective vindication of truth proves to be this humbling sense of the relativity of one's own values in all human relations.

One of the most brilliant strokes in the play is the method Petruchio uses to convince Katharina that no human perspective is absolute. Until she meets him Katharina has been philosophically a monist of an all too familiar kind: there is only one truth, which is known to her and which invalidates all disagreement with her views. A suitor will necessarily submit his will totally to hers because his love will oblige him to recognize her authority. Thus when Petruchio hastens to depart from Padua she says haughtily, "Nay, if you love me, stay" (III. ii. 206). His refusal to accept her rightness merely shows his fatuousness:

> Do what thou canst, I will not go to-day;
> No, nor to-morrow, not till I please myself....
> I see a woman may be made a fool,
> If she had not a spirit to resist.
>
> (III. ii. 210–211, 222–223)

Inevitably Petruchio displays an identical temper—and being physically stronger, his point of view becomes the exclusive one, since he can drag her off. But the point is that Petruchio's physical violence is only a figure for Katharina's psychological brutality; his attitude is a mirror image to Katharina's, and "he kills her in her own humour" (IV. i. 183). Petruchio makes clear that when everything which she feels she deserves is accepted by another person its

refraction through another personality produces exactly the opposite effect to what she expects; for Petruchio in a frank soliloquy
explains that

> amid this hurly I intend
> That all is done in reverend care of her; . . .
> This is the way to kill a wife with kindness.
>
> (IV. i. 206–207, 211)

Indeed, Petruchio's behavior is a triumph of wit—for his
whole courtship duplicates that of an extravagantly sentimental
lover such as Lucentio, whose good sense has been shattered by
sexual passion. In other words, he affects the role of the kind of
lover Katharina would desire, a suitor such as Bianca's. For even
Bianca finds the autocratic manner of her suitors offensive:

> Why, gentlemen, you do me double wrong,
> To strive for that which resteth in my choice:
> I am no breeching scholar in the schools;
> I'll not be tied to hours nor 'pointed times,
> But learn my lessons as I please myself.   (III. i. 16–20)

And, of course, Lucentio's conception of Bianca is exactly as wide
of the mark as Petruchio's affected admiration of Katharina.
"Sacred and sweet was all I saw of her" (I. i. 181), says Lucentio of
Bianca. Yet when he has married her, this little saint ridicules him
for betting on her virtue: "The more fool you, for laying on my
duty" (V. ii. 129).

As long ago as Lucretius and Ovid, such lovers' misrepresentations of their mistresses had been commonplace. The difference between Petruchio's misrepresentations of Katharina's personality and those of other lovers lies not in what he says but in his
consciousness of its inaccuracy:

> I will attend her here,
> And woo her with some spirit when she comes.
> Say that she rail; why then I'll tell her plain
> She sings as sweetly as a nightingale:

> Say that she frown; I'll say she looks as clear
> As morning roses newly wash'd with dew....
>
> (II. i. 169–174)

Petruchio's attitude is thus identical to that of the speaker in Sonnet 138:

> When my love swears that she is made of truth
> I do believe her, though I know she lies.

Quaintly enough, in the play it proves to be the lover who professes to marry for cash and does not necessarily believe the praises he lavishes on his mistress, who achieves a true harmony in marriage and secures a truly devoted woman possessed of the virtues he has mockingly ascribed to her. The skepticism of the mature sonnets is vindicated again.

Of course, Petruchio's satirical conduct does not limit itself simply to the lover's infatuated compliments that ludicrously misrepresent his lady's physique. A true lover also scarcely notices the basic character or even the formal identity of his beloved (as we have seen in both earlier Shakespearean comedies). Thus in pressing his suit he will certainly not notice such relatively minor details as her opinions, even about himself. We all know how incapable lovers traditionally are of recognizing their own unacceptability. Thus Petruchio's obtuseness in not recognizing that Katharina seems to loathe him is true to type. Equally, his extravagant concern for her well-being must always end in her discomfort one way or another if it is to be true to the misjudgments rising from a feeling that nothing is too good for one's beloved. This is a fact which Katharina finally recognizes with real bitterness:

> I, who never knew how to entreat,
> Nor never needed that I should entreat,
> Am starved for meat, giddy for lack of sleep,
> With oaths kept waking and with brawling fed:
> And that which spites me more than all these wants,
> He does it under name of perfect love.   (IV. iii. 7–12)

In contrast to what is usually asserted, the sufferings imposed on Katharina are thus not the result of Petruchio's arbitrary and sadistic whims, nor are they designed simply to humiliate her and ultimately break her nerve. They are systematically calculated to make her aware of the impact of a passionately committed personality on those around him (or her); and the cathartic effect is heightened because the motivation behind their terrifyingly disruptive behavior is his manifest sexual involvement with her, which Katharina has so much desired. It is always a shock to idealists to meet such mirror images of their own fiery temperaments in their greatest admirers; and for Katharina it is doubly disturbing to find that there is "a way to kill a wife with kindness" (IV. i. 211).

Perhaps the situation here may seem too forced and improbable for serious discussion; if so it is worth noting that this weird conflict of wills finds ready parallels in even the most sentimental and attractive love affairs in Shakespeare. Nothing would seem less likely to resemble the harsh battle between Petruchio and Katharina than the pretty encounters of Romeo and Juliet. Yet Shakespeare carefully repeats similar effects in both plays. Compare, for example, the romantic lovers' melancholy aubade after their wedding night with the parallel discussion of Kate and her quarrelsome spouse. Juliet decides that Romeo shall not leave her bed when he chooses:

> Wilt thou be gone? it is not yet near day:
> It was the nightingale, and not the lark, ...
> Believe me, love, it was the nightingale.
>
> (III. v. 1–2, 5)

Romeo disagrees: "It was the lark, ... no nightingale" and points to the rising sun's rays—but Juliet firmly rejects his view: "Yond light is not day-light, I know it, I." Romeo, with the idealistic lover's anxiety to yield everything, accepts her false hypothesis that it is moonlight that he sees, just as Petruchio finally forces

Katharina to agree to whatever astronomical opinion he chooses
to take:

> Then, God be bless'd, it is the blessed sun:
> But sun it is not, when you say it is not;
> And the moon changes even as your mind.
> What you will have it named, even that it is.
>
> (IV. v. 18–21)

Of course, the real difference between the two scenes lies in the
issues involved in the contentions over a verbal point. Kate is smart
enough to recognize fully and finally that mere terminology in
itself is not worth quarreling over. Juliet's momentary stubborn-
ness is potentially far more sinister in its consequences: in making
her assertion about the moon she forgets that if she is mistaken it
could mean the death of her husband for failing to leave Verona by
dawn. Juliet's assertion is thus far more threatening than that of
Kate or Petruchio, and it needs Romeo's open acceptance of his
likely execution to remind his beloved that it is best to assume that
it is dawn, not moonlight, which they see. But Juliet has less chance
to come to any larger awareness in her capitulation. In due course
this fatal clash of perspectives in sentimental lovers will be made
the central motif in the tragedy which befalls Othello and
Desdemona. So the apparently extraordinary discrepancies in
vision between Petruchio and Kate accord perfectly with the examples of more monumental love affairs in the other plays. And if
Petruchio's whims seem merely grotesque, at least they do not risk
the execution of the beloved, like Juliet's, or actually bring it about,
like Othello's.

What Katharina learns from this curious exchange is that all
judgments are relative to the observer—which is not to say that one
has none of one's own, but that this private view can never be advanced as final until the whole network of relationships which
modify and deflect each individual's view of events has been taken
into account. It is with this awareness that Kate now meets the aged

Vincentio. And having learned that the quickest way to achieve her main goal of visiting her father is to humor her husband's minor quirks of fancy, she briskly agrees that the old man is a "virgin, fair and fresh" (IV. v. 37). Forced to reverse her statement immediately, she manages to do so in terms which show how fully she has grasped the way impressions are distorted:

> Pardon, old father, my mistaking eyes,
> That have been so bedazzled with the sun
> That everything I look on seemeth green:
> Now I perceive thou art a reverend father;
> Pardon, I pray thee, for my mad mistaking.
>
> (IV. v. 45–49)

Not only does she handle the situation so deftly that Vincentio relaxes and salutes her as "my merry mistress"; she also manages a series of clever jabs at Petruchio by alluding to the sunlight he was so anxious to call moonlight and blaming herself for a "mad mistaking" which was purely her husband's. She now handles her ridicule of others with a modest efficiency that defies resentment; and she is therefore ready for her climactic triumph, in which she crushes all opposition by affecting the most complete humility. Instead of resentfully beating her sister, she permanently deflates her pretentions to charm; and she totally dismantles the widow's malice without giving her the slightest opening for reply.

Petruchio's role in this last scene of the play has not been adequately understood. It is assumed that he simply glories in having a servile wife. Far from it. Rather, he glories much in her spiritedness, because it is no longer neurotic and ineffective. Instead of being servile or hysterical, she briskly resents the widow's supercilious innuendos, and Petruchio roundly encourages her: "To her, Kate"—"A hundred marks, my Kate doth put her down" (V. ii. 34, 36). The rest of the scene is devoted to the systematic but honorable revenge of Kate and Petruchio on all who have ridiculed their eccentricity. Kate has learned the rules of the social game from Petruchio, and she completely outmaneuvers the opposition by choosing the moderate role for herself. She has understood the truth voiced by Isabella, in her passionate concern for her brother in *Measure for Measure:*

> O, it is excellent
> To have a giant's strength; but it is tyrannous
> To use it like a giant. (II. ii. 107–109)

Katharina argues against the other wives, not as a subjugated and debased woman, but in the full knowledge of her own powers:

> My mind hath been as big as one of yours,
> My heart as great, my reason haply more,
> To bandy word for word and frown for frown;
> But now I see our lances are but straws,
> Our strength as weak, our weakness past compare,
> That seeming to be most which we indeed least are.
> (V. ii. 170–175)

Like Luciana in *The Comedy of Errors,* Katharina now understands that "There's nothing situate under heaven's eye / But hath his bound" (II. i. 16–17), and critics of the play's misogyny would be wiser to recognize that this broader sense of proportion is what governs her final sense of decorum. By assenting to Petruchio's superior resilience and good sense, she vindicates her own. It is precisely this sense of the power gained by proper subordination which causes Milton to make his Christ assert in *Paradise Regained:*

> who best
> Can suffer best can do; best reign, who first
> Well hath obey'd. (III. 194–196)

No one could accuse Milton of thinking Christ's an inferior nature, yet the sustaining power—not to mention the inevitability—of a sense of hierarchy is as essential to him as to anyone. By mere com-

mon sense almost everyone must recognize the superiority of someone else, if not of many others; and the capacity to do so unflinch-
ingly is a symptom of poise and discrimination. Katharina at the
end of the play thus displays all the signs of recovered mental
health.

This certainly does not mean that she is uniformly humble.
A proper contempt governs her judgment on her obtuse companions, and half her pleasure in stressing female subordination lies in
the shock she gives to the smugness of the other wives: "you
froward and unable worms," as she brutally calls them (V. ii. 169).
However, even at this moment she preserves her awareness of the
relativity of values; and her principal emphasis is on her admonition to the other women to recognize that, as with all human
beings, the power of their beauty is no stronger than the credit
given to it by others. If they forget that debt, then they can expect
the penalties she herself has known:

> Fie, fie! unknit that threatening unkind brow,
> And dart not scornful glances from those eyes,
> To wound thy lord, thy king, thy governor:
> It blots thy beauty as frosts do bite the meads, . . .
> A woman moved is like a fountain troubled,
> Muddy, ill-seeming, thick, bereft of beauty;
> And while it is so, none so dry or thirsty
> Will deign to sip or touch one drop of it.
>
> (V. ii. 136–139, 142–145)

Here we have a mind that has fully assimilated and mastered its
own experience. Far from being a servile slave, Kate now clearly
dominates her environment without challenge, as she would have
done from the start if she had deployed her great resources of personality more discriminatingly. She now rules others authoritatively because she in turn may be ruled by superior authority, and
this insures that she will live at peace with those she values highly,
in "love and quiet" and all "that's sweet and happy" (V. ii. 108,
110).

The Taming of the Shrew has usually been dismissed as vulgar farce, and Shakespeare's authorship of it has therefore even been questioned. However, the pattern of its love relationships is unique; their complexity, sophistication, and concern with social propriety could be the product of the author of the *Sonnets* alone. The gifted eccentricity of the principals, the sense of sustained conceptual pressure behind the startling twists of the plot, and the delicate counterpoint of different levels of feeling and of contrasting personalities confronted by the same basic issues—all these display the characteristic organizational powers of Shakespeare, who sustains a far greater range of responses to the issue of love and the mistakes of identity it brings about than Gascoigne, or even Ariosto, is capable of. He restores the coarse realism of Plautine farce which Ariosto had softened; but he also imposes upon all the characters a rigorous pursuit of social accommodation, of a kind with which Plautus rarely concerned himself and which Ariosto only accepts as a final solution to purge the debauched chastity of his heroine (who copulates merrily with her paramour, without interest in the resulting public humiliations for her family). Shakespeare refuses to concern himself with such coarse personalities. Outside the history plays it is the lapses of sensitive minds, not the physical crudities of realized lust, which most concern him. In plays like *Measure for Measure* and *All's Well,* he shows a surprising concern to bed only husbands and wives together in his principal plots. In fact Shakespeare is usually concerned more with the idea of adultery than its actuality—as we see in *Othello, Cymbeline,* and *The Winter's Tale.* Shakespeare refuses to deal with less than the finest failures of the human personality.

It is in this analysis of the best possibilities of human nature that Shakespeare provides the completion of a spectrum largely missing in modern American literature. *The Taming* deals with people who constitute serious social problems: hard-core unemployment and alcoholism in Sly; mercenary egotism in Petruchio; instable youth in Lucentio; sexual sadism in Bianca; above all spinsterish waspishness on the verge of breakdown in Katharina. But the play never afflicts one with that sense of claustrophobic doom with which most modern writers invest their characters. Within the very characters who illustrate the most pernicious traits are found the highest potentials, which are indeed proved to be the correlatives if not the causes of the apparent failures. This is why *The Taming* is so unusually valuable, and it may help explain its modern popularity (even without Elizabeth Taylor and Richard Burton) despite academic critical censure. Katharina is not an unfamiliar figure to us. She is the archetypal gifted woman in an unsympathetic society, but this problem evolves into the even more basic difficulty of any person of talent who finds himself denied adequate recognition. Such people are far more dangerous to themselves and society than is usually recognized, as asserted in Sonnet 94: "Lilies that fester smell far worse than weeds."

Modern educational theory used to meet this challenge by isolating the gifted students. More recent views tend to work toward the social reassimilation of the most and the least gifted, for their own and society's good. Shakespeare provides a template for this process, which startlingly prefigures the means used by the governess in *The Miracle Worker* to enable Helen Keller to realize her potentialities. The instructor refuses to allow the antisocial results of even legitimate self-pity and may properly resort to the harshest and most physical methods if necessary. It is typical of Shakespeare that he shares Thomas Hardy's realism in *In Tenebris II:* "if a way to the Better there be, it exacts a full look at the Worst." Katharina starts by beating up a bound Bianca and is in due course physically assaulted herself. But the end product is the serenely poised matron who definitively puts her malevolent companions in their place without disarranging a hair or displaying a trace of false pride or superciliousness. Unmarried professional women might profitably note her discreet method: only the inconveniences of matrimony normally make it accessible to their sex. To be an adequate professional competitor of the male a woman needs the resources of self-restraint that marriage characteristically affords the male. Only successful marriage can force one to respect the capacities and the limitations of oneself and others. The dashing Don Juan and the intellectual celibate are equally likely to be incomplete human beings, incapable of handling and sustaining worthwhile sexual relationships. Humble matrimony may be a more sophisticated and civilized attainment than either extreme of sexuality is capable of. Katharina both learns and illustrates this fact memorably.

CHAPTER FOUR

Low Love and High Passion

BOTTOM AS ROMEO

SHAKESPEARE surpassed his rivals Greene and Marlowe in part because he was first an actor and knew the possibilities of his medium thoroughly. The same advantage has raised Pinter and Osborne above their present contemporaries, and the lack of it deflected T. S. Eliot's aim at a dramatic climax to his career. Many brilliant insights of subtle Shakespearean critics are marginal; no actor could ever put them across, even to an audience of Shakespearean scholars. Perhaps the effects discerned may be subliminally significant: a minor guarantee that the playwright's intuitions are backed up by all his faculties. But to succeed in communicating, an actor must be more concerned with the explicit motives and actions provided than with overtones audible to perhaps one member in an audience of hundreds. Perhaps the most conspicuous example of this incompatibility of high insights and mere performance can be found in the history of the role of Falstaff. As critics increasingly insisted on the fascinating complexity of Falstaff from the eighteenth century onwards, there was actually a decline in the number of performances of *Henry IV, Part I,* so that the later nineteenth-century London theaters seem positively to be avoiding the play for the most part. Actors and directors wisely chose not to risk snobbish critics' regret of missed yet largely elusive nuances.

Hamlet is now rapidly going the same way: actors are obviously oppressed by expectations about the play which will not let us respond to it simply as a lively and bizarre plot about murder and the propriety of revenge, but insist that every fanciful metaphysical and aesthetic refinement be caught. Perhaps such impossible challenges account for the general turning toward Shakespeare's lesser plays among repertory companies these days. Lesser expectation allows audiences to respond to the characters and story freshly, uncontaminated by nontheatrical scholarly subtleties. For it is the direct, more or less literal response to the spoken word which is the essence of drama, not the intense scrutiny of the study. For this reason all interpretation both on and off the stage must start with a recognition of motives and actions which can be clearly presented and grasped in the theater. Interpretation of *Romeo and Juliet,* for example, might well start from the crude fact that the hero is to be presented as largely responsible for six deaths. Such practical evidence in the play provides a useful pointer to the interpretation that sexual passion is the most deadly force to which naive but gifted young people can be exposed. The increasing deadliness of the violence presented warns us against following the tragic example of Romeo's intense commitment to sexual passion. Thus the play's intended catharsis can be shown to depend on our sympathizing with Romeo's charm and devotion, only to recognize that they serve to heighten the disasters endemic in a turbulent Verona.

Part of the relevant evidence for this interpretation lies in other plays of Shakespeare, like *Othello,* in which the sinister potentialities of untempered passion are stressed by the clear responsibility of that passion for the brutal outcome of the plots. But some of the evidence is simply pragmatic and categorical: sexual passion is wholly corrupting unless redeemed by love. However, perhaps even the divergence between the two terms "passion" and "love" needs to be established for modern readers, who are daily confronted with a semantic garbage heap in which love, sex, charity, passion, and courtesy are all depressingly confused. No better definition of love has been given than St. Paul's. He is talking about relations not between the sexes but between all individuals. However, it is clear that what he requires of men in all relations is what I have stressed as needful in sexual affairs: "If I speak with the eloquence of men and of angels, but have no love, I become no more than a blaring brass. . . . If I . . . hold in my mind not only all human knowledge but the very secrets of God . . . but have no love, I amount to nothing at all. . . . This love of which I speak is slow to lose patience—it looks for a way of being constructive. It is not possessive: it is neither anxious to impress nor does it cherish inflated ideas of its own importance. Love has good manners and does not pursue selfish advantage. It is not touchy. It does not keep account of evil or gloat over the wickedness of other people. On the contrary, it is glad with all good men when truth prevails. Love knows no limit to its endurance, no end to its trust, no fading of its hope; it can outlast anything. It is, in fact, the one thing that still stands when all else has fallen."

The most publicized members of the present generation have little or no sense of this deeply enduring kind of "love." Like Romeo, they accept shallower, more flamboyant standards which are egotistically satisfying but often cruel to others, and usually destructive in the long run. We are told by people like Archibald MacLeish that this kind of hectic idealism proves the worth of the generation now coming to maturity. But such ostentatious virtue is a relapse into the state of mind of the infant, generalizing its selfish needs as cosmic imperatives. The present generation of young people is fortunately not so naive as those melodramatic figures favored by the advertising media; if they were, the best label for them would be not the radical generation but the spoiled one. Nevertheless, to present the hectic incompetence of Romeo or Hamlet as an ideal is to reinforce the worst traits of the present age. The ultimate point about Romeo is not simply that he is so charming but that he is the focus for so much disaster. He is a kind of amatory Ché Guevara, bringing death and destruction to his own cause and allies. Obviously he gets a lot of help in the play from an incompetent older generation; but this excuse and his own good intentions should not blind us to his frequent obtuseness. His naiveté is most plainly revealed by his belief that heightened sexual excitement is the whole of love. Like the drug addict, he thinks that being "high" is objectively as well as subjectively meaningful. Shakespeare understands this feeling, presents it convincingly, but refuses wholly to surrender to it—indeed, he shows that it is often pathological. As his Friar says of it, such passion untempered by love is "bestial" (III. iii. 111); and the treatment of sex in *A Midsummer Night's Dream* is an explicit confirmation of Shakespeare's verdict on the sexual conduct of Romeo.

Some beasts of prey automatically recognize their victims because their prey's flight acknowledges its suitability for attack. Increasingly man's unrefined sexual instincts appear just as primitive to Shakespeare. When he presents naive amatory relationships in the plays of his early maturity he seems to visualize his lovers in the same predatory terms as the ancient Greek poet Callimachus: "On the mountains, Epicydes, the hunter seeks out every hare and the tracks of every deer beset by frost and snow. Yet if someone says, 'See, here a beast is couched' he does not take it. My love is just the same: it can pursue what flees from it, but what lies ready it passes by." It is not accidental that Shakespeare favors Ovid's *Metamorphoses* so heavily as a source of allusion. It is a kind of classical encyclopedia of neurosis and mental disease: Ovid's lists of humans transformed into animals, plants, and objects afford endless equations of pathological states of mind with subhuman forms of existence. The result affords a convenient anthology of morbid case histories for Shakespeare, one exceeding in complexity any modern text available to psychiatry.

Though his basic flaw is egotism rather than passion, Bottom's transformation into an ass when he becomes Titania's beloved is thus a proper figure for Shakespeare's vision of naive sexuality. Shakespeare shows us how undisciplined passion can turn humans into beasts whose sexual reflexes are totally irrational and arbitrary. With this kind of perversity in mind, he makes Helena, a willing victim, exclaim to her alienated lover:

> I am your spaniel; and, Demetrius,
> The more you beat me, I will fawn on you:
> Use me but as your spaniel, spurn me, strike me,
> Neglect me, lose me; only give me leave,
> Unworthy as I am, to follow you.
>
> (II. i. 203–207)

Inevitably this servility fails to trigger the acquisitive sexual instinct of the crudely predatory male; but in passing Helena by, Demetrius only confirms her fixation. Indeed, he pushes it beyond neurosis into suicidal extravagance:

> I'll follow thee and make a heaven of hell,
> To die upon the hand I love so well.
>
> (II. i. 243–244)

The grotesque passion of Titania, the fairy queen, for the assified Bottom is scarcely more perverse.

No significant character in the play is wholly exempt from this sadomasochistic type of sexuality—unless indeed it be Bottom, who has the comparative good fortune to be chiefly devoted to himself: soothed by his own fantasies of mastery he thus articulates his desires without much dependence on others' feelings and largely escapes the emotional entanglements which they get into. By contrast, even Theseus must be recognized as a predatory lover. He shows a certain barbarism when he marries the captive queen of the Amazons, whom he has seized by brute force on the field of battle:

> Hippolyta, I woo'd thee with my sword,
> And won thy love, doing thee injuries.   (I. i. 16–17)

The battle of the sexes can go no further. And the supernatural but primitive world of the fairies displays similar examples of this paradoxical reflex: Oberon quarrels with Titania because he wants her favored boy attendant (whom she in turn stole from the human world), and he only becomes anxious to be reconciled to her when he observes her fatuously in love with another male, whose principal claim to her attention must seem his extravagant inappropriateness as a lover (unless we credit the challenge in the emotional inaccessibility of Bottom's supreme egotism).

A detailed analysis of most of these unrefined passionate relationships in the play seems to suggest an almost mathematical basis for the sexual reflex. Not only are negative emotional values automatically bracketed with positive ones, but any factor reversing the emotional value of a single term in a relationship necessarily also exactly reverses the values of any dependent terms. Lysander thus finds the enforced inaccessibility of Hermia irresistible at the start of the play, while Demetrius is revolted by the surrender of Helena to his suit and inflamed to pathological excitement by Hermia's devotion to Lysander. However, scarcely has Lysander succeeded in making Hermia fully available to himself by their nocturnal flight to the forest than he proves susceptible to the inaccessible attractions of Helena, who has servilely devoted herself to a rival male and thus asserted her total indifference to Lysander. And as soon as Lysander attempts to secure Helena, she proves once more irresistible to Demetrius, who discovers the sign of valid prey in her vigorous resistance to Lysander, which she at once provocatively extends to Demetrius. Of course, the juice of the magical flower which supposedly "produces" these effects is the merest figure for the mathematics of naive sexuality, and Puck's arbitrary administration of it illustrates the accidental quality of the intrusion of passion into human relationships. That the flower is only a dramatic convenience appears in Helena's total revulsion from both her suitors once they avow their new devotion (III. ii. 145 ff.). We can see that her rejection of what she has previously so much desired is precipitated only by the change in others' views, not by magical intervention. Thus the play's fairy world is less an objective force in the plot than a satirical reflection of the fanciful sources of spontaneous human instincts and intuitions. It serves chiefly to make the arbitrariness of human motives more picturesquely explicit, though it can also heighten their best aspects to a healthy ritual magic which reinforces the creative cyclic rhythms submerged in men's nature (compare the disorder described by Titania at II. i. 81 ff., resulting from her quarrel with her husband Oberon, and the play's concluding incantations after marriage has again made sex socially viable).

The human beings initially fail almost entirely to recognize these subliminal elements of experience. Ironically, only Bottom sees the fairies (perhaps as a poet's testimony to the positive powers of supreme egotism). Like *The Comedy of Errors,* the play opens with a lawcourt scene, but one in which legal disciplines confront emotions even more directly than in the earlier play. Initially a sober attempt is made to regulate love by order of the tribunal—the implication of the participants' attempt being that emotion should be subject to reason and systematic analysis. There is an elusive irony in the fact that even the immature lovers victimized by the verdict assume their passion is governed by rational choice. But Lysander nowhere argues more forcefully for this view of passion than after having switched his devotion from Hermia, to secure whom he had faced the magistrate earlier:

> Not Hermia but Helena I love:
> Who will not change a raven for a dove?
> The will of man is by his reason sway'd;
> And reason says you are the worthier maid.
> Things growing are not ripe until their season:
> So I, being young, till now ripe not to reason;
> And touching now the point of human skill,
> Reason becomes the marshall to my will.

> (II. ii. 113–120)

The ratiocinative skill he shows is comparable to Biron's, but it is clearly not exploited with Biron's skepticism, which had prevented him from mistaking plausibilities for facts. Helena has already firmly established for us the irrelevance of objective endowments to a lover's evaluation when she argues that Demetrius switched his affections from her to Hermia with as little justification as Lysander's later reversal of this choice:

> Through Athens I am thought as fair as she.
> But what of that? Demetrius thinks not so;
> He will not know what all but he do know:
> And as he errs, doting on Hermia's eyes,
> So I, admiring of his qualities:
> Things base and vile, holding no quantity,
> Love can transpose to form and dignity:
> Love looks not with the eyes, but with the mind.
>
> (I. i. 227–234)

There is amusing irony in her discovery that she is no happier when she is the recipient of the approval whose lack had so distressed her. Like Katharina's, Helena's wished-for courtship proves a torture, which she feels compelled to blame on pure malice:

> Have you not set Lysander, as in scorn,
> To follow me and praise my eyes and face?
> And made your other love, Demetrius,
> Who even now did spurn me with his foot,
> To call me goddess, nymph, divine and rare,
> Precious, celestial?   (III. ii. 222–227)

It has usually been assumed that all these emotional oscillations are the forced effects in which broad farce usually takes refuge —to be rationalized at best by Theseus in his too familiar and sweeping assertion that

> Lovers and madmen have such seething brains,
> Such shaping fantasies, that apprehend

> More than cool reason ever comprehends.
> The lunatic, the lover and the poet
> Are of imagination all compact:
> One sees more devils than vast hell can hold,
> That is, the madman: the lover, all as frantic,
> Sees Helen's beauty in a brow of Egypt.
>
> (V. i. 4–11)

But we should recognize that Theseus is only one persona among the many vividly animated by the poet in his play. The ruler himself has illustrated the erratic quality which he censures in the other lovers, being attracted to the woman who tried to kill him in armed combat. Indeed, we must regard with some skepticism the judgment of a warrior who not only marries his foe but also trains his hunting dogs so that they are unfit for tracking: "slow in pursuit, but match'd in mouth like bells" (IV. i. 127). Hippolyta opposes his easy judgment that love is wholly whimsical, observing that if analyzed closely the lovers' gyrations prove coherent, indeed systematic, in their illustration of "something of great constancy" (V. i. 26)—as I have already hinted in my mathematical analysis.

In this fashion Shakespeare's "imagination bodies forth / The forms of things unknown." His play as a whole illuminates love's motives better than the supercilious traditional verdict of Theseus on the arbitrariness of lovers. We have already seen that there is a constant in each of the passionate relationships in the play: they all show a resistance to what is available and a desire for what is not. This factor in their choices is unconsciously defined by two of the lovers themselves:

> The course of true love never did run smooth;
> But, either it was different in blood, . . .
> Or, if there were a sympathy in choice,
> War, death, or sickness did lay siege to it,
> Making it momentany as a sound,
> Swift as a shadow, short as any dream;
> Brief as the lightning in the collied night, . . .

If then true lovers have been ever cross'd,
It stands as an edict in destiny.

                    (I. i. 134–135, 141–145, 150–151)

Obviously phrases like "short as any dream" bear on fluctuations of attitude in the play itself, and the total consistency with which obstacles intrude into all the relationships suggests that what is actually involved is not simply the "opposition of the stars" but also the lovers' delight in an emotion heightened by conflict. Passion may indeed be crossed, but the uniformity with which this occurs proves that it is not by chance: the lovers positively solicit difficulty, tension, and separation. Far from resisting the "edicts of destiny," a lover will foster their evil effects with masochistic satisfaction.

Denis de Rougemont has urged the accuracy of such a view of the European amatory tradition in *Love in the Western World;* there he develops his ideas, not in relation to Shakespeare, but by showing the archetypal nature of the endless obstacles which Tristan invents to prevent the serene fulfillment of his passion for Iseult. De Rougemont sees the fear of sustained and disillusioning communion with one's beloved as the motive for the lovers' cult of complications and separation. Divided from the beloved, one is free to indulge in the full sweep of egotistical emotional excitement, uninhibited by the distracting actuality of the beloved's presence. Cressida corroborates this interpretation in her reactions to the counsel of Pandarus after her separation from Troilus:

Why tell you me of moderation?
The grief is fine, full, perfect, that I taste.

                    (IV. iv. 2–3)

If we grant the possibility of such extravagant satisfactions, we see at once that they provide a rationale for the recurring pattern in Shakespeare's portrayal of merely passionate affairs. In his tragedies the lovers' delight in sentimental absolutism proves fatal when untempered by skeptical good sense and the stoic endurance that marks true love. In the comedies the paradoxes of absolutism legitimize the comic reversals and misunderstandings that we have already sampled. The results may be as intense as some of the exchanges between Katharina and Petruchio; or again they may be merely farcical, as in the "tragical mirth" of *Pyramus and Thisbe* which concludes *A Midsummer Night's Dream*. This grotesque interlude is a deft caricature of all the elements that go to make up, the character of the naively passionate love affairs in the play. The disconcerting parallels between *Romeo and Juliet* and *The Taming of the Shrew* have already been noted; but sentimental tragedy is even more strikingly ridiculed in the farcical mishaps of *Pyramus and Thisbe*. Like Romeo and Juliet, Pyramus finds passionate love diminishes his awareness to the point where he can scarcely tell day from night: "Sweet Moon, I thank thee for thy sunny beams" (V. i. 277). Surely Romeo is nearer to Pyramus in such confusions than to the premeditated misjudgments of Petruchio on the same topic. Indeed, the ludicrous behavior of Bottom in the part of Pyramus echoes the antics which the role of even a pretended lover readily imposes on the most opinionated and self-sufficient personality.

In his own character Bottom is fully master of the arts of illusion: in soliciting the various roles in the play (I. ii), his intelligence proves as uncompromised by illusion as that of Theseus often seems. But once he is fully committed to playing the part of Thisbe's sentimental lover, Bottom loses almost all the bluff good fellowship which allowed him to hobnob so merrily with a queen and her fairies. He garbles all his sentiments hopelessly, and in his stilted conduct he resembles Romeo's "fishified" behavior over Rosaline, and sometimes over Juliet. Only the greater detachment of the theater audience from the farce's plot allows them to find Bottom-Pyramus ludicrous when he mistakenly thinks his beloved dead and kills himself. Theseus sees little enough difference between the interlude and any famous tragedy: "The best in this kind are but shadows; and the worst are no worse if imagination amend them" (V. i. 213–214). Later the commentary of Theseus raises even this farcical love affair closer to the level of tragic poetry when he observes of the dead Pyramus that Thisbe "will find him by starlight. Here she comes; and her passion ends the play" (V. i. 320–321). Closer still to the tragedy is the outcome of the misunderstandings: "the wall is down that parted their fathers" (V. i. 357–358). The same climactic resolution of divisions occurs between the Montagues and Capulets after the suicides of their children.

That comical wall itself deserves a little more comment than its quaint manifestation suggests. It is an archetypal image for the obstacle which passion unconsciously solicits as a prerequisite for full ardor. Not only does it provide a concrete analogue to the legal and emotional barriers that create the intensity of all the lovers in the play; it is also a wry distortion of the famous balcony which divides Romeo from his beloved. Just as the balcony fosters Romeo's rhetoric as a sublimation of direct sexual contact, so the farce's Prologue tells us of

> that vile Wall which did these lovers sunder;
> And through Wall's chink, poor souls, they are content
> To whisper. At which let no man wonder.
>
> (V. i. 133–135)

They are "content" with words and separation: this literal meaning is not accidental, as the admonition makes clear. Furthermore, once the lovers uncharacteristically attempt to end their separation, they intensify their own subconscious resistance to genuine mutual involvement. Both readily find excuses for suicide, thus avoiding any need to replace sentimental remoteness with comic realism.

Ironically, the farcical interlude provides the best analogue to the serious tragedy of Romeo and Juliet, for in it Shakespeare seems to be reflecting back sardonically on the theme of "a lover, that kills himself most gallant for love" (I. ii. 25). The farce could have purged excess in the aristocratic Greek lovers who watch it on the stage, but unlike the ultimate audience offstage they fail to recognize in their own roles the grotesqueries which they ridicule in the performance of the lower classes. We know that they have displayed the same love of tension, confusions of perception, and suicidal instincts. However, in the interlude Shakespeare provides even closer echoes for Romeo's and Juliet's behavior and sentiments, implying that the purgative effect which the interlude should have on its stage audience duplicates the cathartic effect *Romeo and Juliet* was intended to have on its actual audiences. Sadly enough, most spectators have also taken at face value the serious play's tragic sentimentality, which Shakespeare's mature comic vision clearly resists and censures.

Just as Russian audiences delighted in the affectations of intellectuals whom Chekhov intended to ridicule, so most English-speaking audiences are as taken in by Romeo's death-dealing charm as Juliet is. They fail to see that as a hero Romeo lies midway between the surrealist horror of the homicidal Richard III, and the bathos of Pyramus. All three lovers exploit language to entrap women who are apparently inaccessible, only to help to destroy them. Like Richard, also, Romeo is a catalyst of disaster, and something close to a mass murderer. He personally kills Tybalt, Paris, and himself, while precipitating the deaths of Mercutio, Juliet, and his own mother. Even before we examine Romeo's character in detail we must keep this simple fact in mind: any character who personally brings about six deaths cannot be simply dismissed as accident-prone. One should also recall Richard's protestations to Lady Anne:

> Your beauty was the cause of that effect;
> Your beauty, which did haunt me in my sleep
> To undertake the death of all the world,
> So I might live one hour in your sweet bosom.
>
> (I. ii. 121–124)

The love of beauty can be literally death-dealing; "fatal passion" is not a figure of speech for Shakespeare.

If it is urged that any comparison between Romeo and Richard III is unfair to the former's innocent intentions, we should note that the evil of an action is not canceled by unawareness in the guilty. Othello is scarcely cleared of murder by asserting, "Nought I did in hate, but all in honour" (V. ii. 295). Nor is Romeo really trustworthy in his protestations. Just before switching his devotions from Rosaline he resists the idea of changing his mistress as confidently as Lysander did before he abandoned Hermia:

> When the devout religion of mine eye
>> Maintains such falsehood, then turn tears to fires:
> And these, who often drown'd could never die,
>> Transparent heretics, be burnt for liars!   (I. ii. 93–96)

Romeo is usually quite humorless, and his lack of the skepticism found in the mature sonnets seems the clearest prelude to a series of failures and disasters comparable to those which befall the hopeful friend of the *Sonnets*. Among the "accidents" that damage Romeo's integrity, nothing is more intrinsic than his breach of faith to his icy ideal, as the Friar stresses for us:

> Holy Saint Francis, what a change is here!
> Is Rosaline, whom thou didst love so dear,
> So soon forsaken? Young men's love then lies
> Not truly in their hearts, but in their eyes. . . .
> Women may fall, when there's no strength in men.
>> (II. iii. 65–68, 80)

Nor does the affair with Juliet show sufficient advance from the earlier affectations to make the relationship viable. We have only to think back to the academic mannerisms of the young aristocrats of *Love's Labour's Lost* to sense the force of Juliet's criticism when she admonishes her suitor: "You kiss by the book" (I. v. 112). She finds it impossible to accept his extravagant protestations of affection, echoing Matthew's gospel (5:34) when she says, "Swear not by the moon," "Do not swear at all," "Well, do not swear" (II. ii. 109, 112, 116). Instead of seeing love as an opportunity for emotional rhetoric, she sees it as the occasion for a significant social contract; she is concerned to know whether "thy bent of love be honorable, / Thy purpose marriage" (II. ii. 143-144). She thus shares the sentiments of the cycle's opening sonnets (which were written about the same time), agreeing with their sense of man as a part of society rather than as an egotistical mystic.

But Romeo is too often insensitive to such discriminations, which might have validated and preserved his new relationship. For him beauty is valuable only as a transcendental essence; what he admires would be debased by earthly utility:

> O, she doth teach the torches to burn bright!
> It seems she hangs upon the cheek of night
> Like a rich jewel in an Ethiope's ear;
> Beauty too rich for use, for earth too dear.
>
> (I. v. 46–49)

Throughout the play he vigorously resists the idea that he might live to enjoy the company of Juliet in a full and fruitful relationship:

> come what sorrow can,
> It cannot countervail the exchange of joy
> That one short minute gives me in her sight:
> Do thou but close our hands with holy words,
> Then love-devouring death do what he dare;
> It is enough I may but call her mine.
>
> (II. vi. 3–8)

Romeo appears here complacently to anticipate disaster.

Indeed one wonders whether the supposed perfection of a given moment does not foster the death-wish, as Othello is so unexpectedly to reveal after recovering his bride from the threat of a storm at sea:

> O my soul's joy!
> If after every tempest come such calms,
> May the winds blow till they have waken'd death! . . .

> If it were now to die,
> 'Twere now to be most happy; for, I fear,
> My soul hath her content so absolute
> That not another comfort like to this
> Succeeds in unknown fate.   (II. i. 186–188, 191–195)

With the hindsight resulting from our knowledge of Othello's attitude and crimes, we may also be more inclined to recognize such an unconscious bent toward disaster in Romeo's behavior. Like Lysander and Hermia, Romeo tends to blame fate for the misfortunes of "true love" when indeed his own state of mind is largely responsible. Having killed Tybalt in a fit of reaction against the high-minded intervention which clumsily provoked the death of Mercutio, Romeo exclaims, "O, I am fortune's fool" (III. i. 141). But it is he who has duped himself by preferring the delusions of high sentiment and intense passion to the humbling realities of sustained social intercourse.

Like the undirected intelligence of the aristocrats in *Love's Labour's Lost,* the picturesque poetry and romantic enthusiasm of Romeo cannot be cherished for their own sake without monstrous impropriety. The alter ego of Romeo's excessive exaltation appears in his relapse into murderous violence: "Fire-eyed fury be my conduct now" (III. i. 129). And of course that violence is suicidal, as the Friar sharply observes:

> Hold thy desperate hand . . .
> Hast thou slain Tybalt? wilt thou slay thyself?
> And slay thy lady too that lives in thee,
> By doing damned hate upon thyself?
>   (III. iii. 108, 116–118)

At best, like so many modern young rebels, Romeo is an unconscious conspirator with Fate against himself; at worst he takes conscious satisfaction in misfortune: "How oft when men are at the point of death / Have they been merry!" (V. iii. 88–89). Since the most excitingly intense feelings and idealizations are generated by impediments to love, and since the supreme impediment to love is death, unqualified passion solicits the death of both the beloved and the lover. Thus the supreme moment of exaltation will be fixed immutably without further demeaning effort. If the lover is to gain immortality as a secular saint, he must attain the fixity which martyrdom reassuringly confers on a saint before religious beatification. No less than the deliberate religious martyr, Romeo is thus necessarily the enemy of life, and even of sexuality in its physical forms.

For it is not accidental that *Romeo and Juliet* is one of Shakespeare's more explicitly obscene plays. Only the intransigent virtue of Angelo and Isabella can polarize sexuality and sentiment more disturbingly. There is a poetic truth in the observation that Romeo's idealism must kill off Mercutio's hearty realism, which threatens to transmute it into something less exciting and more practical. Each of Romeo's idealistic flourishes provokes an obscene riposte from his friend that conceals a lesson Romeo needs to learn. Mercutio and the nurse display all that practical awareness of the physiology of sex which Romeo ignores as totally as Biron's companions do:

> Romeo! humours! madman! passion! lover!
> Appear thou in the likeness of a sigh:
> Speak but one rhyme, and I am satisfied ...
> This cannot anger him; 'twould anger him
> To raise a spirit in his mistress' circle
> Of some strange nature, letting it there stand
> Till she had laid it and conjured it down;
> That were some spite: my invocation
> Is fair and honest, and in his mistress' name
> I conjure only but to raise up him.   (II. i. 7–9, 23–29)

Romeo never manages to express so openly the physical aspects of his love either for Juliet or for Rosaline. In neither case does he even mention any explicit desire or capacity to enjoy these physical phases of love for which Mercutio is the spokesman, not even after his supposed wedding night.

Indeed, Romeo unwittingly allows himself to serve as the representative of sexually inhibiting forces, suavely corrupting Juliet's practical nature with his poetic sentimentalism, and accidentally destroying those who, like Mercutio, cherish fertility and reproduction. His actual conduct presents a harsher version of the friend's resistance to marriage in the *Sonnets*. The death of Juliet after a single night of love is thus not pathetic but a warning of the dangers of high sentiment, for she is at first largely on the side of marriage and physical sexuality. Unlike Romeo, who neglects these aspects of sex, she looks forward impatiently to the physical consummation of her marriage, asking Night to

> Hood my unmann'd blood, bating in my cheeks,
> With thy black mantle; till strange love, grown bold,
> Think true love acted simple modesty.   (III. ii. 14–16)

She is eager to lose maidenly reserve in favor of the fullest sexual consummation, which Romeo seems almost anxious to ignore and avoid. The heart of the tragedy lies in Romeo's involuntary subversion of this vital principle epitomized by his bride. Increasingly she too becomes addicted to the manic-depressive cycle of her "beautiful tyrant, fiend angelical" (III. ii. 75). Their very first contact leaves her a prey to the classic tension which Shakespeare associates with sentimental extravagance:

> My only love sprung from my only hate!
> Too early seen unknown, and known too late!
> Prodigious birth of love it is to me,
> That I must love a loathed enemy.   (I. v. 140–143)

She also dwells on thoughts of the time "when he shall die" (III. ii. 21), finding a heightened exhilaration in the universal annihilation of death.

However, such manifestations of unbalance are far less characteristic of Juliet, and it is appropriate that she first takes refuge in feigned death rather than the actual suicide into which Romeo precipitately plunges himself. She is finally conquered (like Cleopatra) less by her own hastiness than by the irresistible example of her beloved. Indeed, it may be said that Juliet's tragic flaw lies chiefly in her susceptibility to the immature aspects of Romeo's passion, and his in the failure to participate fully in the comic awareness which he helps to extinguish in Mercutio. Sexuality must prove a tragedy to those who cannot attain the poise of the speaker in the final sonnets, a lover who blends stoic acceptance of misadventure with witty skepticism about his beloved and himself. Only thus can lovers defeat "reckoning time, whose million'd accidents / Creep in 'twixt vows" (115). To describe Romeo as unqualifiedly excellent is to favor love's defeat and death. No doubt the wiser mood in which to leave the play is the sobering one of Theseus: "in the night, imagining some fear, / How easy is a bush supposed a bear!" (V. i. 21–22). If we are made to sympathize with Romeo's commitment, it is only in the end to realize the more emphatically the incompleteness of his awareness of the nature of matured love. The play may be a tragedy of passion, but it is not really a tragedy of true love, for such love, by Paul's definition and the standards of the *Sonnets,* is too patient to betray itself into tragedy.

Because of its more varied and witty exposition of this issue, *A Midsummer Night's Dream* may claim to be a maturer, if not a richer, play than *Romeo and Juliet.* In it the potential tragedy of ideal love is recognized and overcome by a lifegiving sense of the comedy of sexual relations. Instead of the simple polarizations of the tragedy (young against old, sentimental enthusiasm against practical satisfaction), the comedy has Shakespeare's characteristic range of illustration. This variety results in a subtler kind of characterization. Because there are so many pairs of lovers, the limitations of the purely subjective view of sexuality are comically visible, and we are not overpowered by a single narrow perspective as we may well be in the tragedy. The virtuosity of the structure of the *Dream* has long been noted and praised, but its worth lies, not simply in the skill with which all the plots are interwoven, but in the way that interweaving allows juxtapositions which comment on the conduct of the individuals involved in each sequence. Above all there is one figure, Bottom, who exists on every level of reality in the comedy. Sustained only by his self-assurance, he moves coolly through his ludicrous metamorphoses, from his "realistic" role as an urban craftsman to the more sophisticated one of actor; and then from involuntarily playing the monstrous lover of the Queen of the Fairies to his own choice of tragicomic role as the Romeo of a classical romance.

Theseus behaves with aristocratic propriety throughout the play, but I think that as a model for most moderns the lower-middle-class Bottom is the more relevant figure. He accepts the idiotic roles afforded or thrust on him by the play with a good will and even satisfaction that never run to complete self-deception. When Titania dotes on his ludicrous charms, he accepts her "love," but he also wryly comments: "Methinks, mistress, you should have little reason for that: and yet to say the truth, reason and love keep little company together now-a-days; the more the pity that some honest neighbours will not make them friends" (III. i. 145–149). In such moods of rueful acceptance he comes nearest in the play to the skeptical yet committed mood of the speaker in the *Sonnets*.

It may be argued that a literary critic has no business pointing out the practical moral of such works and holding up Bottom to the young as at least partly a worthy model. But it seems unlikely that Shakespeare would show us on his stage an audience of young lovers smugly failing to grasp the intended ridicule of themselves implicit in *Pyramus and Thisbe* without being aware of his own impact on actual audiences. In other plays also, like *Love's Labour's Lost,* he shows stage spectators lacking in the discriminations about spectacles they are watching within their own play, which Shakespeare thus stresses to his own audience. In both plays the witty young gallants are over-concerned with the polish and refinement whose lack arouses them to a contempt for Holofernes and his coterie scarcely less than that shown for Bottom's troupe. The wits fail to take into account the substance of the performances they ridicule, and miss the social and ethical implications in the failures of pretentious sentiment, at least insofar as they reflect on the wits' own previous lapses in the same direction. Within his plays Shakespeare shows us that art can function as "a criticism of life" (in Arnold's fine phrase). For this reason I feel that critics are justified in making explicit the ways in which Bottom's enactment of the role of Pyramus reflects not only on Lysander but also on the related role of Romeo.

Bottom is important as a model because he is not trapped in any role and accepts each only as long as it seems worthwhile to those around him. Such flexibility and responsiveness are the marks of true sophistication (as we see in Falstaff), and that sophistication is not completely invalidated by its coexistence with all kinds of plebeian mannerisms and grotesque quirks of egotism. Most audiences have still to be shown that while we can allow ourselves to sympathize with Romeo and thus learn vicariously from his incompleteness, we might well positively admire Bottom's diverseness and emulate his poise, while laughing at his egotism. As a model he is at least as plausible and perhaps more impressive than such a modern analogue as Joyce's plodding "anti-hero" Leopold Bloom. Whether most young women would want Bottom rather than Romeo as a lover is debatable; but this is their misfortune, at least if we credit what Shakespeare shows happening to those of his comic heroines who prefer more superficially charming but less flexible spouses than Bottom, like Bassanio, Orlando, and Bertram. It requires all the mental agility of Portia, Rosalind, and Helena to avoid Juliet's fate and to instill something of Bottom's bemused, comic acceptance of his various roles into their well-meaning but tragically sincere young mates. Each of Shakespeare's mature comedies displays in detail how to complete the task of sexually educating the immature male once you've caught him, a process which is only begun at the end of *Love's Labour's Lost*. It proves to be a far more dangerous business than the mere taming of a shrew.

TRIANGLES IN THE SONNETS AND
"THE MERCHANT OF VENICE"

We can no longer respond to *The Merchant of Venice* as Shakespeare intended, because nowadays we tend to identify men more by their involuntary attributes than by their chosen identities. Earlier ages did not feel it worth recording that Augustine was dark or Cleopatra blond (as they probably were). It is left for modern, racially-inclined scholarship to insist that the key to *Othello* lies in the supposed Elizabethan view that Moroccans were prone to jealousy. Similarly we are told that the portrayal of Shylock proves Jews were held to be sadists. But it does not follow that we must simply read *The Merchant* as the story of how a gang of complacent Christians cruelly turn his own weapons against a neurotic Jew, whatever the feelings of Shakespeare and his contemporaries may have been. The analogy between the "plot" of the *Sonnets* and the triangle of Antonio-Bassanio-Portia is close enough to recall that the tensions between the friends in the *Sonnets* needed no mere villain to provoke them. As with the earlier comedies, we would do well to modify the ethnic view of *The Merchant of Venice* by assuming that the bizarre difficulties which it portrays rise from the excellence of its antagonists, not their defects. What distinguishes Shylock from the other Venetians is not so much his surface Jewishness as his unique precision in social relationships. If anything, he shows in this a kind of "tragic virtue" (an idea that might help us to reverse our conception of the supposedly flawed nature which a modern perversion of Aristotle's archaic doctrine of heroic error has also imposed on Shakespeare's tragic heroes). Equally, the mental posture of Shylock's competitor, Antonio, is too complex to permit us to see him simply as the unfortunate innocent. He is something more relevant to modern states of mind.

Indeed, the first lines of the play suggest that it is anachron-istic to read it as a dogmatic assertion of the superiority of the Christian temperament. It is true that throughout the play Antonio is praised in terms comparable to Bassanio's partial account:

> The dearest friend to me, the kindest man,
> The best-condition'd and unwearied spirit
> In doing courtesies, and one in whom
> The ancient Roman honour more appears
> Than any that draws breath in Italy.
>
> (III. ii. 295–299)

Salerio corroborates this: "A kinder gentleman treads not the earth" (II. viii. 35). But Shakespeare shows us also that a man so liberally favored with virtue can be deeply tainted with neurosis from the very start, before misfortune strikes:

> I know not why I am so sad: . . .
> And such a want-wit sadness makes of me,
> That I have much ado to know myself.   (I. i. 1, 6–7)

Here is a figure not unlike Herzog: a victim almost consciously in search of disaster. Later Antonio's welcoming of his fate is almost more masochistic than stoic:

> I am a tainted wether of the flock,
> Meetest for death: the weakest kind of fruit
> Drops earliest to the ground; and so let me.
>
> (IV. i. 114–116)

The self-censure exceeds even the humble self-sacrifice of the speaker in the *Sonnets,* and Antonio is more than capable of com-parable self-destructive devotion to a friend. His response to Bassanio's request for further assistance in his courtship of Portia is of an absoluteness which modern attitudes might only dismiss as affected if the modern Jewish novel had not made clear its latency in the most sensitive men of our own age:

You know me well, and herein spend but time
To wind about my love with circumstance;
And out of doubt you do me now more wrong
In making question of my uttermost
Than if you had made waste of all I have:
Then do but say to me what I should do
That in your knowledge may by me be done,
And I am prest unto it.   (I. i. 153–160)

It is essential to Shakespeare's meaning that we link this extreme of devotion and humility with Antonio's melancholy. Like so many modern American intellectuals, the high-minded speaker of the *Sonnets* had found the failures of the world intolerable in the face of his high expectations: "Tired with all these, for restful death I cry" (66). Even the unique compensatory excellence of his friend ultimately fails him. As with the protagonist of the *Sonnets,* Antonio lives by his fanatic devotion to the ideal. This longing for perfection inclines him to transfigure his chosen friends to divinities for whom all must be endured, but to debase the merely painstaking virtue of Shylock to vicious egotism meriting the harshest censure. In the confrontation between Antonio and Shylock we find the archetypal clash of Mary and Martha: the heroic improvidence of supreme devotion challenged by the pragmatic realism of respectful good sense.

If this were the whole of the story, we might indeed resentfully agree with the facile assumption that the play intends to demonstrate the superiority of the Christians' sentimentality, and resent its denigration of Shylock's dutifulness. But we must note the characteristic doubling of Shakespeare's resources which allows him to transfigure his models. From the start the dramatist demonstrates that Antonio's philosophy of life is not practical, as Gratiano briskly observes:

You look not well, Signior Antonio;
You have too much respect upon the world:
They lose it that do buy it with much care.
                                         (I. i. 73–75)

In repudiating calculated decorum in favor of passionate devotion to the ideal, Antonio condemns himself to perpetual misery. His friend must fail of the perfection required of him, and the hatred which Antonio's contempt has generated in Shylock carries for Antonio its legitimate penalties of continuous emotional strain (if not of death). Far more than the earlier comedies, this play dramatizes the inner principle of the *Sonnets,* that the extravagant love of the Good is disastrous.

We are never in doubt that Antonio's treatment of Shylock is an aberration. He continually uses phrases of inhuman harshness to Shylock (just like any modern radical addressing a policeman or Southern politician citing legal precedents for his actions):

> Mark you this, Bassanio,
> The devil can cite Scripture for his purpose.
> An evil soul producing holy witness
> Is like a villain with a smiling cheek,
> A goodly apple rotten at the heart:
> O what a goodly outside falsehood hath!
>
> (I. iii. 98–103)

And when Shylock protests at having been called "dog" (compare today's "pig"), Antonio superciliously responds, "I am as like to call thee so again" (I. iii. 131). This is the voice of hubris, of Lear confidently judging Kent, or Othello, Cassio. Any idealism which fosters such savagery is partly barbaric, as the city of Berkeley now knows to its cost. And the specific inadequacy of Antonio's sentimental outlook appears in the impossibility of regulating all one's social relations by it. There is deliberate irony in the fact that it is precisely Antonio's devotion to Bassanio which condemns him to the loveless contract with Shylock. Antonio finds that, far from being able to live by pure affection, affection is what commits him to inhuman contracts, as he admits to Shylock:

> If thou wilt lend this money, lend it not
> As to thy friends.   (I. iii. 133–134)

Antonio thus contemptuously insists on the most inhuman kind of contract, indeed suggests to Shylock that it be framed to recognize their deadly opposition. The fatal pact is thus not simply the product of Shylock's bitterness; Antonio positively solicits it. The relevance of all this to contemporary life is obvious: idealistic absolutism is still provoking its enemies to do their worst.

Shylock's conduct also demonstrates that one becomes what one hates. Ostensibly Shylock favors the maintenance of social decorum (not to say "law and order") at any emotional cost to the individual, rightly esteeming that the broad sweep of human interrelationships in a society as complex as Venice cannot be regulated simply by private feelings, whatever Antonio thinks. Thus he strives resolutely to disguise and suppress his personal resentment in the early scenes. That it is visible at all constitutes a failure in self-discipline which itself reflects on the inflexible standards to which he also adheres. In his devotion to them he is as capable of self-abasement before an enemy as Antonio is before a friend. There is little to choose between them at this level. And Shylock's failure in maintaining commercial decorum is no less significant than Antonio's double betrayal by his friend Bassanio (who commits him to Shylock and then fails to preserve him). For Shylock's hatred bursts through his commercial realism. Christians have so unnerved him by their cult of feeling that he cannot resist a bitter wager against its adequacy, ironically couched in their own sentimental terms. The contract is by no means intended simply in the murderous way it superficially reads. Shylock is mocking Christian devotion in requiring the security of a pound of flesh; for what he is asking of Antonio is that, in trusting to Bassanio, Antonio risk his heart. If Bassanio proves an unworthy friend, Antonio will thus both literally and metaphorically lose all heart, as Shylock says: "I will have the heart of him, if he forfeit" (III. i. 132). Antonio, too, recognizes how deeply the penalty for Bassanio's heedlessness will cut: "I'll pay it presently with all my heart" (IV. i. 281).

The implications of the contract are thus far deeper than the

merely sadistic ones of the agreement in the play's source. Shakespeare constructs his action to demonstrate that a friend will not
only dissipate one's fortune but also, at a pinch, forfeit one's heart
and life in pursuit of his own selfish sexual gratifications, just as
the friend did in the *Sonnets*. No wonder Antonio is in tears when
he sends Bassanio off to court Portia (II. viii. 35–50), for the intuition of betrayal is inevitable in a man of Antonio's subtlety, just as
it was for the speaker in the *Sonnets*. The penalties of this contract
are at least as severe for Shylock. Having surrendered to emotion at
the cost of commercial decorum, he finds himself publicly trapped
in a tragic commitment no less pathetic than Antonio's, for all that
it is a surrender to hate rather than to a sweeter emotion. Neither
Antonio's overt love nor Shylock's repressed hate is compatible with
sustained social relationships, however virtuous both ways of life
may seem.

The same point about the insensibility and tactlessness of dev-
otees of passion is made, with delicate variations, by the ancillary
details of the plot. The minor theme of Jessica's elopement with
Lorenzo illustrates the ease with which humane values get lost in
the excitement of headstrong sexual involvement. Most audiences
must sympathize with Shylock when he laments that the pair of
eloping lovers have swapped his stolen engagement ring for a
monkey (III. i. 113–128); and even with each other, the lovers soon
fall from sentimentality to somewhat malicious mutual banter
(III. v. 88–96; V. i. 12–23). But, of course, the courtship of Portia
provides the balancing sexual variant of the theme of love for Antonio's devotion to Bassanio, just as the Dark Lady occasioned the
evolution of the awareness of the nature of friendship in the
Sonnets. Nor is this courtship's import on the feeling between the
Venetian friends limited to the forfeit of the contract. The false
choices made by Portia's suitors reflect directly on Antonio's devotion to Bassanio. Just as Jessica takes on extra charm for her lover
when she "gilds" herself with ducats (II. vi. 49), so Antonio's
wealth to begin with commands Bassanio's full attention to his

friendship; but once this is taken advantage of, Antonio is largely forgotten in favor of a sexual satisfaction reinforced by Portia's larger dowry. Thus the golden casket wrongly chosen by the Prince of Morocco epitomizes the range of motives linking most other characters in the play, even perhaps Shylock and his daughter. Though he starts from different premises, the Prince fails, just like Antonio and Shylock, to handle the full range of motivation.

Equally, the silver casket preferred by the Prince of Aragon carries a larger relevance in its misleading inscription: "Who chooseth me shall get as much as he deserves" (II. ix. 50). Like this Prince's, Antonio's fate proves "much unlike my hopes and my deservings" (II. ix. 57). Bassanio recollects his friend's worth only after having doomed him by negligence. Shylock's humiliations are no less at odds with his rectitude. A leaden casket is thus the only suitable symbol for the results of human affection and virtue: all excellence implies leaden moods, and even perhaps coffins (as in *Romeo and Juliet*). This imagery ultimately works the opposite way from Bassanio's expectations: he may at first appear to win handsomely by suspecting showiness, but he nevertheless fails to expect his own impending miseries. He is immediately denied the consummation of his fortunate marriage by his realization that it has betrayed him to public shame in abandoning his friend to death. And thereafter he discovers that he has been made a cuckold before he has even bedded his bride (not unlike Othello, and Claudio in *Much Ado*). These misfortunes remind us that Bassanio wins Portia more by her prompting than by his insight. His deplorable failure to handle his emotional obligations soon becomes obvious, even to him:

> How much I was a braggart. When I told you
> My state was nothing, I should then have told you
> That I was worse than nothing; for, indeed,
> I have engaged myself to a dear friend,
> Engaged my friend to his mere enemy,
> To feed my means. (III. ii. 261–266)

It should be clear that Bassanio's surface charm and sensitivity mask a nature as volatile and immature as Romeo's. Both show the characteristic power of Shakespeare's lovers to rationalize fickleness in appealing terms: by being true to the moment they are false to ultimate truth. Perhaps nothing better illustrates Bassanio's superficiality than his conduct in the famous court scene. By this time Antonio has come to recognize the need for the impersonal regulation of human conduct which Shylock in his wiser moments stands for; he accepts his own misfortune rather than seek a specious exception from the law:

> The duke cannot deny the course of law:
> For the commodity that strangers have
> With us in Venice, if it be denied,
> Will much impeach the justice of his state;
> Since that the trade and profit of the city
> Consisteth of all nations. Therefore, go.
>
> (III. iii. 26–31)

We see at once the relevance of Portia's outlandish suitors: they too accept the intolerable obligations laid on them, because negotiations between different value systems require the assent to conventions alien to either or both, if any profitable relations are to ensue. Antonio is thus taught the logic of public restraint at the expense of private commitment and the perfect propriety of Shylock's mode of business.

But when we compare this recognition with Bassanio's behavior at the trial we discover that he still displays the same mixture of sentimentality and special pleading which vitiates the early phases of other Shakespearean love affairs, and none of the final decorum of Portia's other, rejected suitors:

> I will be bound to pay it ten times o'er,
> On forfeit of my hands, my head, my heart:
> If this will not suffice, it must appear

> That malice bears down truth. And I beseech you,
> Wrest once the law to your authority:
> To do a great right, do a little wrong.   (IV. i. 211–216)

The moral insensibility revealed here is also reflected elsewhere, as Bassanio consistently "rectifies" one mistake by proposing another, often more disastrous. Having failed to dismantle the legal system which embarrasses him, he tries to offset his failure in devotion to his friend by gross protestations of loyalty which the unrecognized presence of his wife only serves to make more contemptible:

> Antonio, I am married to a wife
> Which is as dear to me as life itself;
> But life itself, my wife, and all the world,
> Are not with me esteem'd above thy life:
> I would lose all, ay, sacrifice them all
> Here to this devil, to deliver you.   (IV. i. 282–287)

This is the impotent rhetoric of a guilty conscience that has lost control of the situation it has precipitated. Shakespeare is very careful to stress Bassanio's feebleness at this point, above all by allowing Portia to comment on her new husband's hopeless confusion of loyalties:

> Your wife would give you little thanks for that,
> If she were by, to hear you make the offer.
> (IV. i. 289–290)

Gratiano's wish that his spouse were dead caricatures Bassanio's offer, but it confirms that Gratiano's superficiality differs only in degree from his friend's: both are still volatile to a potentially disastrous extent. Significantly it is Shylock who has the authoritative comment on such a society as Venice's:

> These be the Christian husbands. I have a daughter;
> Would any of the stock of Barrabas
> Had been her husband rather than a Christian!   (IV. i. 295–297)

Of course, we should remember that Shylock's own rigor had earlier caused him to wish that "my daughter were dead at my foot" (III. i. 91). Ultimately, we must judge all the male figures in the play as erratic, because of their excessive commitments to onesided views of experience. In this they are no less plausible than the characters in the earlier comedies.

But *The Merchant of Venice* enriches its plot with a subtler characterization than any of the earlier comedies. Each character is more delicately balanced between good and evil, and the humor is sadder than before. The play is far nearer to the realism of *Measure for Measure* than to the fun of *The Taming of the Shrew,* because of its legalistic confrontation of moral dilemmas and the ritual severity of its purgation of its characters' vices. Obviously, Antonio's idealization of his friend costs him as complete an acceptance of imminent death as Claudio's in *Measure for Measure.* The idealistic Antonio is forced to assent to the value of Shylock's code, even while being destroyed by it, a concession never exacted yet of opponents of "law and order." On the other hand, Shylock is forced to recognize that only by assenting to the Christian principle of mercy can he or any other man hope to survive the full rigors of the law to which he is so devoted. If he insists simply on Old Testament righteousness, he must be executed at his own insistence: this surely is the moral of his "conversion." The dilemma is one that his legalism precipitated, and his tormentors merely objectify it; his acceptance of life implies rejection of the *lex talonis* of the Old Testament. The moral is that attacks on society based on the demand for absolute rectitude must necessarily backfire because they invite scrutiny of the attackers' conduct by the same standards.

For Bassanio the humiliations are less acute but more shameful and protracted than those inflicted on his more consistent elders. He is publicly shown to have abandoned his friend and then symbolically to have repudiated his wife by disposing of her ring at his friend's discretion (shades of Freud and *The Story of O!*). The climax of the play in Belmont cannot be the serene idyll some superficial readers make of it. Rather it is carefully designed to submit Bassanio to the ultimate catharsis of public humiliation for the betrayal of his most intimate relationships. He is forced to make a flat confession of his untrustworthiness:

> If I could add a lie unto a fault,
> I would deny it; but you see my finger
> Hath not the ring upon it; it is gone.
>
> (V. i. 186–188)

One should note the unintended overtones of Bassanio's confession: he implies that only the physical impossibility of concealing the loss of the ring forbids him to lie about it. Given the chance of successful deception, he seems to say, he would take refuge again in the evasions which have precipitated disaster throughout the play. More comic purging seems almost inevitable for a character still capable of such obtuseness of manner.

The first stage of his renewed expiation lies in Portia's sadistic promise to duplicate his erratic fancies, sacrificing all normal relationships to the pursuit of the sentimental whim of the moment. He put caskets before bodies, rated friendship more than marriage: she will give her body for her ring and express her gratitude for Antonio's salvation by as complete a sacrifice of her marriage as Bassanio had been willing to make to pay for Antonio's safety:

> Let not that doctor e'er come near my house:
> Since he hath got the jewel that I loved,
> And that which you did swear to keep for me,
> I will become as liberal as you;
> I'll not deny him anything I have,
> No, not my body nor my husband's bed.
>
> (V. i. 223–228)

The eccentric sexual gesture Portia here pretends she will make helps us to understand the peculiar climax of *The Two Gentlemen of Verona*, where Valentine offers to prove the genuineness of his reconciliation with his unstable friend Proteus by giving him Valentine's own beloved, Silvia, whom the now repentant Proteus had previously attempted to rape. Obviously even in that early play Shakespeare had been fascinated and amused by the weird consequences of literally carrying out the extravagant commitments affected in naively intense friendships. Thus Portia demonstrates that the insane logic of untempered devotions leads directly to rationalizations for their exact opposite: undiscriminating sexual promiscuity. Once again the naively ideal and the crudely obscene prove as inseparable as in *Romeo and Juliet;* only a saner compromise can reconcile the sentimental and the physiological aspects of sex in a healthy and stable relationship.

Neither Bassanio nor even Antonio has yet fully grasped the limitations of his unqualified idealism, its unconscious proneness to vicious practices. Antonio backs up Bassanio when he resorts to more protestations of future perfection:

> Portia, forgive me this enforced wrong;
> And, in the hearing of these many friends,
> I swear to thee, even by thine own fair eyes,
> Wherein I see myself—   (V. i. 240–243)

Such continued insensibility needs a brutal shock if it is to be restored to good sense. Therefore Portia exploits her last resource: "Pardon me, Bassanio; / For by this ring, the doctor lay with me" (V. i. 258–259). This equivocal truth finally reduces the specious Bassanio to shamed silence. With symbolic appropriateness he now seems to have lost a body (his wife's) in expiation for once having seemed to forfeit his friend's to Shylock. Of course, both are only apparent misfortunes, so all ends happily, with the hope that the men have been purged of some of their earlier extravagance.

One is left to note that the role of Portia in all this resembles Petruchio's in its superiority to conventional insensibilities and incompetence. Like Petruchio, she is largely a surrogate for the dramatist in the manipulation and purgation of the other characters. She it is who saves Bassanio from becoming another Romeo. But unlike Petruchio, she is shown to have earned her poise by her discreet accommodation with her father's will, since it required so fantastic a mode of courtship. Despite her passion for Bassanio (betrayed so charmingly in her famous Freudian slip of the tongue, III. ii. 14–17), she toughly reins in her instinct to violate the arbitrary formulas imposed on her by her father's authority. She has the skeptical wit to see that appearances are deeply misleading—but that this tendency may be as much a force for good as for bad. While Antonio, Shylock, and Bassanio bring disaster by pursuing the good too undiscriminatingly, Portia proposes to all of them sufferings of the most horrific kind, which prove as evanescent as their momentary recognition is therapeutic. Portia is thus the mask for Shakespeare himself. She accomplishes for the cast what the dramatist hopes to achieve in his audience: a comic purge of the obtuseness innate in idealism, through a tempestuous vision of conflicting goods.

It is most important to note that here (as in many of his comedies) the infinite kindliness of Shakespeare requires that he carefully arrange the plot to avoid any material damage even to the slightest of his fictitious characters. Antonio suffers no loss of his ships or life and displays his deepest kindliness even to his Jewish enemy, by restoring the substance of his wealth to Shylock. In assenting to the principle of charity that spares his life, Shylock regains his fortune for himself and his daughter. Bassanio finds his wife chaste despite the truth of her apparent avowals of promiscuity. Resentful modern responses to the play are thus largely false to its spirit and intent. Because of our own idealistic obtuseness and prejudice we tend to intensify some elements unduly, above all the racial tension around Shylock, while playing down compensating elements that might damage our own self-esteem, such as Antonio's neurosis and Bassanio's specious insensitivity.

This triad of unbalanced males must be carefully weighed against each other by any discriminating modern director. Instead of making Shylock's Jewishness an excuse for a lot of easy local color, Shylock's temperament should be exactly weighted against Antonio's neurasthenia, so that the sufferings of Antonio become fully as dramatic as Shylock's. And the emotional climax of the play should lie in Bassanio's bizarre humiliations in the fifth act. For Shakespeare, this tempering of the amatory pretensions of the romantic male who causes all the trouble must be the ultimate goal of his play. Belmont will thus not seem so much a final magical escape from reality as the place where truth finally breaks through to rectify the sentimental illusions, first of Portia's suitors, then of all the Venetians. There the play's last bawdy exchanges will restore copulation to its rightful central place in sexual relations. A little earlier Lorenzo's affectation of high sentiment may seem to open that last act with an appearance of exquisite romance, but close attention reveals that these allusions are at least potentially ominous: Cressida and the fall of Troy, the fatal misunderstandings of Pyramus and Thisbe, the suicidal melancholy of the abandoned Dido. Like much exposition of Shakespeare's sexual themes, a purely romantic reading of the scene seems to dissipate his intended effect upon his audience. Shakespeare surely does not simply favor the idealizations that can destroy life; rather, he shows that they must be tempered to accommodate the matured, good-natured skepticism which alone seems to sustain human relationships.

Properly produced, *The Merchant* is thus a play which displays the self-deceptions of emotional commitment not only in sexual but also in social and legal terms. The imaginary world in which these misjudgments are rectified by patient effort and witty intelligence is obviously not really Venice (or London), but it is closer to our own in the complexity and bitterness of the issues presented than that of the *Dream*. Understandably it was one of the earliest of Shakespeare's comedies to receive intensely serious analysis. However, the implications of Portia's confrontation with Shylock should not be isolated from the whole, or his sufferings stressed at the expense of those of Antonio and Bassanio, which are no less intense and appropriate. It is their comparable misjudgments and incomplete vision which bear most on our modern narrowmindedness. Our refusal to see exactly why their punishment is morally justified and corrective probably rises from our unwillingness to censure the practical inadequacy of Antonio's solemn cult of selflessness and our nervousness at the thought of admitting that the immaturity of Bassanio's behavior is not a lapse in Shakespeare's tact but truly representative of the author's considered verdict on the ambivalent behavior of any romantic male untempered by experience. The best corroboration of this skeptical intent is to see how the role of such naive male figures darkens in Shakespeare's succeeding comedies.

ROSALIND, HELENA, AND ISABELLA:
THE DESCENT TO SEXUAL REALITIES

Rosalind is Shakespeare's most delightful heroine, and her sexual experience anticipates the vagaries of our own age closely. Shakespeare's other female characters may be more passionate or heroic, more deeply moving to the audience, but Rosalind experiments most successfully with the range of amatory relationships open to both sexes. Her capacity for bisexuality seems to impress Shakespeare greatly, for he never shows her less than creatively alert and responsive to all the nuances of amatory feeling and action that surround her. By the end of *As You Like It,* her sexual insights are so potent that she anticipates Prospero's magical dominion over his environment: "Believe then . . . that I can do strange things . . . and yet not damnable . . . though I say I am a magician" (V. ii. 63 ff.). However, she is never tyrannical in her authority over others' emotions. By comparison even Portia has a strain of the termagant (one might even say of the racist) in her contemptuous attitude to her foreign suitors, not to mention her cat-and-mouse treatment of Shylock and Bassanio. When Rosalind finally resolves all the emotional tangles which have grown up around her because of her fascination for both sexes, it is without false rhetoric or drastic action. Simply because she is able when she wishes to present herself as what she most conveniently should be, all the problems evaporate into mere absurdity. As a catharsis of incompetence in her victims this is one of the least painful in the comedies. Rosalind is thus all a woman can ever hope to be. Emotionally committed to femininity yet sexually experienced in both male and female attitudes, she remains witty and skeptical enough never to be trapped in an inexpedient role. She thus deserves our closest attention as the most successful model for women in Shakespeare.

She is the more impressive in that her proficiency is less artificial than that shown in the manipulations of any of the earlier comedies. In Petruchio we encountered a fascinating but enigmatic figure whose therapeutic operations on Katharina's responses obviously depend directly on Shakespeare's own sophisticated awareness. Unfortunately there is no more attempt to explain how Petruchio might have acquired this invaluable finesse than to justify the extraordinary intellectual superiority of Biron over his more academic companions in *Love's Labour's Lost*. By contrast, it is true that the peculiar marital settlement imposed on Portia by her father's will offers a strengthening challenge to her personality, which may help to explain her dominion over her companions in *The Merchant of Venice*. But the evolution of Portia's personal awareness is far less evident and instructive than Shakespeare's delicate exposition of Rosalind's maturation. Far from centering on clever permutations of the pastoral mode, *As You Like It* is concerned to explore the crystallization of personality by building up a scintillating constellation of human types centered on Rosalind's own kaleidoscopic identity. Here for the first time we see a womanly figure plausibly capable of attaining St. Paul's heroic ideal of "being all things to all people."

At the start of the play Rosalind displays a gifted character in equipoise. Despite her dependent position since the exile of the duke, her father, she has learned how to accept her misfortunes "as one, in suffering all, that suffers nothing" (*Hamlet,* III. ii. 71). Indeed, the superiority this gives her to her friend Celia, daughter of the usurper, soon so infuriates the envious father that he banishes Rosalind for her very merits:

> She is too subtle for thee; and her smoothness,
> Her very silence and her patience
> Speak to the people, and they pity her.   (I. iii. 79–81)

She herself was previously so aware of the perfected stasis of her way of life that she coolly considered the idea of deliberately losing emotional balance for the fun of it. Seeking to "devise sports" to distract her mind, her first inquiry is: "What think you of falling in love?" (I. ii. 27). Love for her is thus to be the same kind of testing game that wrestling physically is for her more naive lover, Orlando.

We therefore find her even keener than Juliet to respond to the cleverly varied claims on her sympathy with which Shakespeare endows the conventionally romantic figure of Orlando. Her surrender to love is more consciously explicit and candid than any other heroine's:

> He calls us back: my pride fell with my fortunes;
> I'll ask him what he would. Did you call, sir?
> Sir, you have wrestled well and overthrown
> More than your enemies.   (I. ii. 264–267)

For the less experienced and humorous young women in most of Shakespeare's plays, such a surrender leads directly to disaster. With Juliet, Hero, Cressida, or Desdemona, the frank avowal of love for a genuinely respectable man brings about their ruin. Nor is the exile of Rosalind immediately thereafter an exceptional release from pressure. Most of Shakespeare's romantic heroes escape their beloved's presence with the assistance of authority (though all find themselves inconveniently restored to their ladies' company earlier than they might have wished, at least subconsciously). Rosalind really escapes disaster more creatively, and the way she does so takes us back to the theme of Sonnet 94, the capacity to keep one's deepest feelings to oneself. Rosalind's flight in male disguise is her salvation, even though she still risks the paradoxical misfortunes of Helena and Hermia by sharing her lover's refuge in the forest. Fortunately he is too intoxicated with passion to identify her accurately. Her own drastic reversal of sexual roles serves by contrast to crystallize fully her awareness of the arbitrariness of the human lot, which the play commemorates so schematically in Jaques' speech about "the ages of man." Far more than Jaques, Rosalind is forced to surrender her established identity wholesale to the demands of threatening circumstances. Jaques merely affects to don the clown's motley, which his whimsical egotism has anyway largely earned him. But by disguising herself as a boy, Rosalind has to give up that very sexual pattern to which she has just committed herself in her avowal to Orlando.

It is this chastening of her sexual identity which makes Rosalind so interesting to moderns, for whom her ambivalent experience has become increasingly familiar in both sexes. We now are accustomed to trousered women and effeminate males. Rosalind's experiments as a male are an early prefiguration of Jung's sense of the creative possibilities of at least some awareness of bisexuality. In her exchange of sex we see how a maturation of personality like Katharina's or Isabella's might be achieved without the arbitrary intervention of a magician like Petruchio or Duke Vincentio. Nor is this tempering process merely a latent theme in the play. Intending us to recognize fully how Rosalind attains that dazzling sexual finesse which finally allows her to secure the happiness not only of herself but of all the lovers in the play, Shakespeare permutes the sexual roles of Rosalind with a virtuosity exceeding that of a Petronius, or a Boccaccio, or even a Proust.

These roles of Rosalind require her portrayer to be a youthful

Proteus, for her changes of identity are paradoxical in the extreme. We must start from the inescapable fact for an Elizabethan audience (as with a recent authentic London production of the play): they are watching here a boy actor playing a girl's part, a fact Shakespeare insists on our recognizing also in Rosalind's Epilogue ("If I were a woman . . ."). Thus the play cannot invite us to see a realistic display of how women behave, with all their conventional lapses into human fallibility (such as Chekhov's *Three Sisters* shows us). Rather, it presents a girl's role boldly illuminated, heightened, even transcended, by exploitation of the unconventional vigor and wit that a boy must almost inevitably bring to it. Shakespeare's comic heroines (and Rosalind *par excellence*) thus map out the way for truly emancipated modern women to behave, precisely because these roles were *not* originally to be acted by women but by unusually vivacious males. The parts necessarily lack the easy sentimentality and the merely physical eroticism which all too often resulted from the introduction upon the stage of actresses (and hence of traditional ideals of femininity) in facile roles of the kind sometimes evident in the plays of Dryden, or even Wycherley.

Moreover, in *As You Like It* the boy originally playing Rosalind appears physically costumed as a girl only three brief times in the play. For Shakespeare's tact usually disdains to exploit any direct demonstrations of sexuality. All the physically erotic passages in his presentation of amatory themes are retrospective, and often second-hand. The physiological fascinations and sexual capacities of such women as Cleopatra or Imogen are necessarily narrated, often by other characters than their lovers (such as Enobarbus or Iachimo). Still more than theirs, Rosalind's role as a young woman is deliberately deprived of even a retrospective physiological interest: she is costumed as a boy and "her" maleness is even finally acknowledged openly in the play's epilogue. By means of such devices "Rosalind" is forced to adopt a pattern of purely mental or inward femininity (which is, after all, true to the discipline of the actor playing the part). Further, the actor is obliged to sustain "her" feminine nature while continually performing in situations more appropriate to male virility, such as responding to the blunt erotic advances of the nymph Phoebe or playing a sexually jaded Mercutio to Orlando's sentimental Romeo.

The surface form of this latter relationship of Rosalind with Orlando marks one of the most bizarre extremes of Shakespeare's sophistication of personality: the boy actor here plays a girl who is continually playing at being a boy, who in turn has to humor Orlando and "pretend" to be the girl (Rosalind) that he is supposed, by the conventions of the play, actually to be. The role of Rosalind thus dissolves into a chromatic spectrum of personae. As a boy actor she speaks as a male in the Epilogue; as avowedly a girl she speaks to Orlando in Act I, scene ii, only for a few moments; as a supposed male she masquerades as Ganymede thereafter, except when she "falsely" affects to be feminine for Orlando's instruction. Shakespeare produces many interesting results from this detachment of a rational mind from its wildly oscillating sexual identity. He suspends Rosalind's awareness precariously between the two poles of human eroticism formed by the conventional roles of men and women. As a maturing person, Rosalind eagerly investigates both sexual potentialities; and Shakespeare shows us this process with an assurance modern writers have only recovered since Jung asserted the presence of both the female-oriented persona (or anima) and the male animus in all human personalities, whatever their local physiological attributes.

From a very early moment Rosalind begins to analyze her relationship to her various sexual roles. She even starts out briskly by claiming many of the physical capacities of a male:

> Were it not better,
> Because that I am more than common tall,
> That I did suit me all points like a man?
> A gallant curtle-axe upon my thigh,
> A boar-spear in my hand; and—in my heart

Lie there what hidden woman's fear there will—
We'll have a swashing and a martial outside,
As many other mannish cowards have
That do outface it with their semblances.

(I. iii. 116–124)

The choice is a common one for Shakespeare's women, always
with tragic results if it is made without Rosalind's cool suspicion
of affected virility. St. Joan and the Duchess of Gloucester (in
Henry VI) both mistake the toughness and bellicosity of the male
for absolute virtues, an error far more subtly developed in the
character of Lady Macbeth. Rosalind, by contrast, does not ape
the male out of envy, but through mere necessity. And in mas-
querading as a man she comes to recognize that what conventionally passes for virility is often little more than her own masquerade.

By virtue of that disguise she also acquires an insight into
male psychology uncolored by the effects of sexual excitement.
She can speak to Jaques, Silvio, and Orlando with the privileged
bluntness of a fellow man when she sees their behavior uncen-
sored by awareness of a female observer. Even more instructively,
she is forced to recognize and cope with the classic aberrations of
women's sexual behavior without the advantage of a softening
screen of male sentimentality. She discovers not only much to reproach in the perverseness of her lover Phoebe, but also in herself.
Moreover, her own wayward instincts can find no release with
Orlando beyond their own censure in her objective exposition of
women's responses to courtship (III. ii. 360 ff.). Rosalind's detachment from her identities is a magnificent school for self-awareness, as well as a unique pedagogic opportunity in her dealings
with others. As with Prospero's feigned tempest, Rosalind is able
to stage-manage a storm of emotional entanglements, confident
of her power to resolve them because she is sharply aware of their
artificiality and arbitrariness.

Phoebe is thus brought down from her role as Silvio's cruel
deity by public proof that she is so indiscriminate as to focus her

own sexual interests on Ganymede, a person not only physically unequipped to meet them, but indeed scarcely actual in any way at all. Orlando is purged of a lover's sentimental affectations by relentlessly authoritative instruction in female unpredictability. Paradoxically, he comes to know the nature of his mistress fully just because for a time he fails to recognize her as other than a discriminating friend. But of course the play's most creative display of personality development lies in showing what all this complication does to Rosalind and what she makes of the result, for she alone in the play (except, perhaps, for Jaques) knowingly develops her own nature by deliberate choices.

Early on in the forest her responses oscillate, and her estimates of her own nature are quite contradictory. On the one hand she asks: "Do you not know I am woman? When I think, I must speak" (III. ii. 263) and on the other, she asserts to Orlando: "Me believe it! you may as soon make her that you love believe it; which, I warrant, she is apter to do than to confess she does" (III. ii. 406–408). The latter passage has the ingenious dramatic irony so characteristic of Shakespeare. A mere two hundred lines of dialogue have advanced Rosalind from sentimental confusion at the approach of her lover ("Alas the day! what shall I do . . .") to wry self-judgment. The fatuous example of Phoebe's treatment of Silvio further increases her detachment from the conventional role of a mistress, while the whimsical egotism of Jaques' humor ("a melancholy of mine own . . . in which my often rumination wraps me in a most humorous sadness" IV. i. 15 ff.) serves as a further awful example of the dangers of complacency.

Thus, in affecting to flirt maliciously with Orlando, Rosalind attains a dual catharsis: enjoying perhaps a vestigial and harmless delight in female waywardness, yet also dramatizing for herself a role that she sees to be frivolous if not contemptible. As one such scene develops, one notes how its tone delicately evolves. Rosalind's contempt for her lover's rhetoric becomes explicit: "These are all lies: men have died from time to time and worms have eaten them, but not for love" (IV. i. 106–108). But at the same time, she progresses from affected flirtation to a far less flippant rehearsal of the marriage ceremony (with the comment, "There's a girl goes before the priest; and certainly a woman's thought runs before her actions" IV. i. 139–141). Obviously Rosalind is no longer simply illustrating attitudes which she plans to reject, she is also experimenting with the as yet merely hypothetical marriage contract which she will soon be ready to carry out in practice. In her play she is preparing for a role which she will soon adopt in full earnest, even though surely never at the expense of her liveliness ("the wiser, the waywarder" IV. i. 162).

As in all Shakespeare's comedies, the surface humor of *As You Like It* rises from the ridiculous behavior produced by intense emotions untempered by good sense. But more than most, the play organizes these eccentricities into a complex investigation of the interaction of the conscious mind with its emotional drives and the physiological equipment with which it finds itself arbitrarily endowed. The other characters in the play are merely the resultants of exterior pressures triggering predictable responses. They are "but stewards of their excellence," ultimately guided to their own well-being largely by the will of Rosalind. She alone explores her own identity, faculties, and roles with creative intelligence.

Just as interesting is her healthy respect for danger. Knowing the limitations of herself and others, she has a practical caution that her naive lover Orlando cannot attain. When he optimistically tries a fall with Fate in the person of the wrestler Charles, his brother has insured that the stakes are life and death; Rosalind risks only an emotional pang when she risks a fall with Love. She arrives in the forest well provided and is soon comfortably established in a cottage. Orlando arrives penniless and starving: he has to demand food at sword's point from the outlaws, again no very wise proceeding. Later he also attacks a hungry lioness. For all the witty lectures he receives from Rosalind, Orlando shows no clear symptoms of maturity. Indeed, his own sexual desire is largely a conventional reflection of Rosalind's spontaneous interest in him.

If, as I believe, the distinction of drama lies in its capacity to show broadly meaningful changes in situations and characters, then *As You Like It* depends for its importance almost entirely on the role-changing of Rosalind. And in this it is a work of consummate virtuosity, for Shakespeare manages to convince us thoroughly of the plausibility of her emotional growth to womanhood, from her initial unawakened state, through casual sexual excitement, to wry self-awareness and tough recognition of her lover's conventionality, to which she reconciles herself in marriage. If I had my way the play would be required reading for every teenage girl, not as a charming pastoral fantasy about outlaws and country pleasures, but for this successful exposition of what the sexual maturing of feminine temperament ideally should be. The rest of the play may be charming or merely clever, but as a whole its richness and importance depend on its principal female role.

Rosalind's career shows that young women who emulate the roles of their male contemporaries can only learn the inadequacy of such models. We see the greater richness of a realistic feminine perspective which is undistorted by sexual envy of the male with all his greater capacities for physical folly. However, any modern mass attempt to imitate Rosalind may well still favor coeducation—not as a means of assimilating the sexes, but as an occasion to dramatize their intrinsically contrasting natures. A boyish girl may well be amusing for a time and learn from her experience, but if she matures into a mannish woman she risks becoming a monster—not because women cannot compete with men, but because the conventional Anglo-Saxon ideal of male excellence is an inferior type of personality in itself.

If there is a single Shakespearean play which captures the tensions produced in society by such shallow male stereotypes, it is *All's Well That Ends Well*. This is a play which in many ways corroborates the ideas of *As You Like It* by transposing its sense of the corrective role of female sexual authority from a world of pastoral charm to one that closely reflects the sordid realities of contemporary experience. Like *Measure for Measure, All's Well* has alienated bardolaters because the attack on sentimentality and romanticism latent in the earlier plays is now made fully and unavoidably explicit. While one may distract oneself from Romeo's limitations with the help of his poeticisms, Shakespeare makes it impossible to pretend that Bertram's egocentricity is anything but obtuse, uncouth, and self-defeating. Despite its relentlessness, the play is performed nowadays with increasing frequency, often in modern dress; and its heroine Helena not only appealed to the Romantic poet Coleridge but also served as the major prototype for the Shavian heroine who dominates such successful modern plays as *Man and Superman* and *St. Joan*.

Ironically, the play's basic story line may faintly remind us of a fairy tale like *Cinderella:* a humble but gifted girl manages to make a dazzling marriage with the aid of a miracle or two. However, the relentless success with which she tracks down, captures, and finally subdues the will of her reluctant spouse has more in common with Ibsen or Strindberg than with Shakespeare's conventional contemporaries like Lodge (who provided the material for *As You Like It*) or Greene (who developed the Elizabethan characterization of vivacious heroines). *All's Well* shows how the irresistible power of a determined and capable personality can reach into the recesses of volition of the conventional egotistical male, dominating even the act of orgasm itself. Compared with the sinuous capacities of a fully aware woman, Bertram's flight from his wife in naive pursuit of the thrills of irresponsible philandering and Italian wars proves the veriest adolescent escapism. It is in the interest of society as well as of

Helena that such a dangerous personality as Bertram's be removed from circulation and recycled or neutralized as soon as possible.

Helena is one of the most interesting of all Shakespeare's heroines even though superficially she is the avowed model for the aggressive females molded by Shaw's sexually eccentric personality. Hitherto, Shakespeare's mature comedies have been dominated by women like Rosalind and Portia, whose charm survived the possession of minds superior to the erratic males with whom they had to deal. But before creating these women he had dealt with harsher personalities, like St. Joan, Queen Margaret, and Katharina. In Helena we catch Shakespeare combining these more realistic studies of gifted women and a harsher view of male psychology to create a comedy which proves far less gay than the brilliant successes of Portia and Rosalind. In curing the king's disease Helena may show the almost magical manipulative faculties of these two heroines, yet she finds their effective application on other occasions as painful and almost as costly as the dangerous insights of Desdemona or Cordelia. Shakespeare is now beginning a deeper exploration of his previous idea that a dominant woman is likely to be a destructive force, rather than a creative influence, in a truly contemporary society.

Nothing could better illustrate the gifts of Helena and the sordid world in which she has to apply them than her early comments on Parolles, the scurrilous companion of her beloved Bertram:

> One that goes with him: I love him for his sake;
> And yet I know him a notorious liar,
> Think him a great way fool, solely a coward;
> Yet these fix'd evils sit so fit in him,
> That they take place, when virtue's steely bones
> Look bleak i' the cold wind: withal, full oft we see
> Cold wisdom waiting on superfluous folly.

(I. i. 109–115)

Rosalind is never forced to make so harsh yet maturely tolerant a judgment, just as she never has to face the sexual scurrility of Parolles' advocacy of female debauchery (I. i. 134 ff.). Rosalind may tease Orlando about male affectations of passion, but her satire of his sentimentality is merry innocence in comparison with Helena's bitter recognition of her husband's arbitrary promiscuity in which he unknowingly has sexual intercourse with her, his repudiated wife, while thinking her to be his new mistress.

> O strange men!
> That can such sweet use make of what they hate,
> When saucy trusting of the cozen'd thoughts
> Defiles the pitchy night: so lust doth play
> With what it loathes for that which is away.
>
> (IV. iv. 21-25)

Helena's evolution thus takes her deeper into awareness of human viciousness than any of Shakespeare's comic heroines have gone since the misjudgments of Adriana, the lively if shrewish wife in *The Comedy of Errors.*

Like Adriana too, Helena is a more convincing personality because she is not the instrument of some superior mind (as is Katharina, for example). Her insights result plausibly from her own dangerous initiatives, which she takes with more realistic awkwardness than the almost incredible tact shown by Rosalind. A gifted woman is more likely to find herself in Helena's embarrassing position in proposing to her unwilling suitor Bertram than in the comfortable role of the other comic heroines, whose lovers fail to resent (or even perceive) their own humiliating entrapment. True, Bassanio suffers only the appearance of cuckoldry in his wife, and he appears to choose Portia himself earlier, though in fact he is merely acting out her diplomatically oblique instructions in so doing. No doubt also Helena could hardly make her choice public at the king's behest with more diffidence:

> I dare not say I take you; but I give
> Me and my service, ever whilst I live,
> Into your guiding power. This is the man.
>
> (II. iii. 109–111)

More than any earlier Shakespearean heroine, Helena has reached this moment of sexual truth by incredible effort and ingenuity; but there is irony in the total irrelevance of this excellence to the arbitrary sexual inclination of her fiancé, which he usually dignifies by the name of love.

This public confrontation boldly raises questions which have little of the outwardly comic about them. Despite the king's insistence on rewarding Helena's cure with a husband of her own choosing, Bertram bitterly denies the acceptability of an arranged marriage, no matter how worthy a bride may be who comes so authoritatively recommended by a benevolent sovereign. He insists on his right to passionate choice, either by mystical intuition or an involuntary excitement, rejecting the willed reconciliation of contrasting personalities which I have called love. However, when the king brusquely condemns Bertram's preference for more spontaneous motives, saying, "Thou wrong'st thyself, if thou shouldst strive to choose" (II. iii. 153), we must also wryly reflect that if Bertram is unwise to favor casual sexual attraction over objective merit in choosing a wife, Helena is soon proved equally wrong in choosing exclusively on the basis of her own sexual desire; for Bertram justifies the worst censures passed on him as "a foolish idle boy, but for all that very ruttish" (IV. iii. 242). Parolles's sneering comment is confirmed both by Bertram's fellow officers (IV. iii. 1 ff.) and by his total incompetence in choosing friends and dealing with his wife and mistress. The last scene of the play exposes Bertram to the most abject public humiliation (not, incidentally, unlike what will historically befall Shakespeare's own son-in-law, Thomas Quiney, many years later). Bertram appears first as a liar and a murderer, then as a man who cannot even tell which woman he has made love to. Can anything be more destructive of human dignity than for him to listen to the revelation of his unconscious use by his wife as a mere engine, to produce a pregnancy he has consciously opposed?

We may understand Bertram's helpless capitulation to his wife's will after such total entrapment, but we must also certainly recognize that this final resolution of the conflict has nothing comic or gay about it. The male will is destroyed; the female triumph leaves Helena little room for sentimental idealization of her beloved. Love of a purely romantic kind is discredited on both sides; of itself sexuality has shown that it can be merely something mechanical and without any necessary positive meaning. This new marriage is stripped of its two false if conventional resources, mutual respect and meaningful bodily satisfactions. What is left is to build up a realistic relationship founded on the resigned tolerance which society extends even to such an outcast as Parolles: "though you are a fool and a knave, you shall eat; go to, follow" (V. ii. 57–58).

Such truly Christian charity leaves little room for gaiety, and if the play is a comedy, that is more because of the virtuosity with which it dodges impending disaster than because of any delightful exercise of wit or fancy. Of its principal humorist, Parolles, the best that can be said is that "he hath outvillained villany so far, that the rarity redeems him" (IV. iii. 305–306). Placed firmly in a plausible social setting, Shakespeare's comic love motifs readily darken toward tragedy. Whether in Ephesus, Padua, or Rousillon, his sense of sexual relations transmutes the quaint traditional comic apparatus of mistaken identities and sentimental extravagances into a series of harsh misjudgments which corroborate all too well the need for the skeptical detachment in love of the later sonnets. Where such massive insensibility (not to say incompetence) can occur, the mature mind does not seek to judge, merely to avert irreversible choices:

> Our rash faults
> Make trivial price of serious things we have,
> Not knowing them until we know their grave:
> Oft our displeasures, to ourselves unjust,
> Destroy our friends and after weep their dust:
> Our own love waking cries to see what's done,
> While shameful hate sleeps out the afternoon.
>
> (V. iii. 60–66)

The response of many male readers to this play is extremely self-betraying. They cannot endure the thought that it represents Shakespeare's considered view of the basis of most enduring sexual relationships: the rescue of a blundering sentimentalist from his tragic follies by an increasingly skeptical and pessimistic beloved. Indeed, for most people Helena's Machiavellian gambits are barely redeemed by her good intentions and self-sacrifice. But Bertram seems to them quite deplorably unrepresentative of the young male. Yet if we compare him with the other young Shakespearean heroes who play more attractive roles it turns out that their conduct is sometimes comparable to Bertram's. Romeo abandons Rosaline for Juliet without a qualm and falls to brawling on the day of his marriage, with consequent exile from his new wife, whose supposed death he precipitates. Hamlet rejects Ophelia and drives her to madness and suicide after killing her father without reason and then abruptly leaving for foreign parts. Bassanio offers to give his new wife's life up to Shylock in exchange for Antonio's. Orlando runs away from the court where he has just fallen in love with Rosalind and fails in due course to recognize her as the pretty boy in the forest.

What critics dislike about *All's Well* is thus not simply the detailed behavior of Bertram, since they accept that as more or less understandable in other figures. It is that Shakespeare decides to drop the other heroes' more charming attributes. For once, the naked truth about adolescent passions is objectively presented without any of the offsetting virtues which make the behavior

of a Romeo tolerable. In a modern dramatist like Pinter or Osborne such severity of presentation is usually seen as a positive
achievement, and I am reassured to find that the play's acceptance by most modern audiences suggests that in practice the universality of the relationship between Helena and Bertram is increasingly recognized.

With *All's Well* we have necessarily come close to the end
of Shakespeare's comic investigation of sexual attitudes. Its definitive explicitness suggests that the rich variety of the romantic
comedies has finally been subjected to a formal discipline un-
palatable to many agnostic readers: that of the medieval morality
play. This makes *All's Well* a blunt conclusion for the sequence
of comedies, one analogous to that provided for the tragedies by
the severities of *Timon*. However, there remains one Shakespearean play of this period which achieves a technically comic resolution for sexual aberrations and which seems to me even more
decisive in its implications than *All's well*. *Measure for measure*
presents us with a vision of Renaissance Vienna as an urban society which is as physically decayed, as morally decadent, and as
ripe for champions of "law and order" as present-day Chicago,
New York, or San Francisco. Its police force is shown to be frequently brutal and corrupt, its women are unchaste or neurotic,
and the leaders of its political establishment are mostly shifty,
supercilious, and unfeeling. Venereal disease is as rampant in this
Vienna of Shakespeare as it is in Governor Reagan's California.
The institution of marriage is collapsing, and its jails are crowded
with violent alcoholics like Barnadine or slanderers of the rulers
like Lucio.

Here we find a society even more sleazy, corrupt, and insensitive than that to which Shakespeare transposed his gifted
heroine in *All's Well*. But in Vienna not only have we lost the
ambiguous charm of Belmont and Arden; we also find the gifted
woman stripped of any masking picturesqueness of mind or body.
Isabella is not witty, and she is sexually insensitive, not to say

obtuse. Her mind has a certain harsh vigor and she can be trained to react discriminatingly. But her personality is potentially as neurotically destructive as Katharina's. She presents merely the raw material of a gifted personality. Her erratic puritanism and emotional stiffness are the corollaries of the debauched society in which she finds herself. She herself cannot assimilate physical sexuality to her ideas or personality in any way, and the play couples the sexual faculty with either brutally commercial prostitution or the pangs of unwanted and dangerous pregnancy. The women in the play are either superciliously religious, prostitutes, or unwed mothers, and none are more charming than the pimps, murderers, and corrupt officials who represent the male sex. In every case of interest we are presented simply with unsexed intelligences having various physical apparatuses, male and female, more or less at their disposal, though these organs are also subject to a coarse sexual chemistry beyond the possessors' control.

Idealization of sexual relationships is almost inconceivable in such a world where even simple social contracts between the sexes are not viable. We are now confronted by an image of the Fallen World as we ourselves know it, and Shakespeare offers us not the least shred of romantic consolation. Any remaining gaiety is literally either gallows humor or sick jokes derived from the diseases of the brothel. Shakespeare has thus set himself the final test dramatically which he had set himself lyrically in the last sonnets. Rejecting all romantic aspirations, he asks: What can be built from the chaos inevitably produced by sexual instinct, and the resulting neurotic repression of it, both subjective and social? Curiously enough, his answers on both levels are as hopeful as in all his previous comedies, if not more so. Sex proves to be a catalyst not only of evil but ultimately also of awareness generally, as long as hysteria and extreme solutions are avoided.

Once again it is through the creatively ambivalent feminine role of his principal boy actor that Shakespeare chooses to display the climactic accommodation of the free human will to the dis-

locating imperatives of sex. At the start of the play, the outstand-
ing male figure, Angelo, shares with Isabella a confident detachment from the destructive passions that afflict baser human
natures. As the new governor appointed to clean up Vienna,
Angelo undertakes as relentless a chastening of the body politic
as Isabella does of her own body in becoming a novice in a religious order. By the same paradoxical insight which undercut the
excellence of the friends in the *Sonnets,* Shakespeare makes Isabella's aggressive virtue the agent for the destruction of the complacency of all his principals in the play.

Despite her hysterical puritanism (precipitated no doubt by
the ubiquitous depravity of Vienna), Isabella finds that her love
for her brother enforces on her a plea for Christian mercifulness
even though his capital offense is a sexual lapse of the kind she
abhors. There is the more irony in her situation because it is the
whispered promptings of Lucio that spur her in her pleas for her
brother's life, for Lucio is habitually given to that sexual viciousness which surrounds her. Thus the universality of sexual depravity at least teaches virtue the need for mercy. Isabella is necessarily
accusing herself (albeit unconsciously) when she reminds Angelo:
"Why, all the souls that were were forfeit once" (II. ii. 73). Her
own confidence that she can persuade in swaying Angelo must
rest largely on her awareness of possessing that "prone and speech-
less dialect, / Such as move men" (I. ii. 188–189) which Claudio
intends her to use against Angelo. In the end she frankly admits
that she helped to corrupt Angelo into his attempt to debauch her:

> I partly think
> A due sincerity govern'd his deeds,
> Till he did look on me.   (V. i. 450–452)

Nor does she scruple to use the body of Angelo's ex-fiancée
Mariana as a replacement for her own in order to entrap Angelo
once he has become fascinated by her own personal virtues.

Thus the intense pressures of amoral sexual desire bring

about the dislocation, but also the rehealing and ultimate recovery of flexibility, in those human personalities that the play first shows to us petrified by their own stiff sense of virtue. In these self-discoveries the more or less innocently Machiavellian duke has no deep emotional involvement; he serves only to provoke and sort out the tangle of the plot a little improbably by a few brisk jerks at the end of the string. It is the emotional unbalance of the other characters which is the true source of action. For all the sexually active personalities in the play (Angelo, Isabella, Mariana, Claudio, Julietta, Lucio, and others), sex functions as a brutal and indeed often a near-fatal catharsis of personality, one reminding them of the artifice both of their own private identities and of their social roles. Isabella uses her femininity to hypnotize Angelo while pleading for mercy to lechery only to find that if this fault may be excused in her brother she cannot in turn herself be plausibly quite so morally indignant at Angelo's sexual advances; and she soon allows herself to sink to the role of procuress for others in order to escape from her personal ethical dilemma. Cruder humiliations befall each of the other hopefuls.

Altogether the play reflects a savage vision of the texture of human society, one scarcely less harsh than that of *Timon* or *King Lear;* and it also shows the virtuous in all their neurotic fixity. Even the duke, surely a surrogate for the playwright's manipulating hand, shows no endearing traits. Yet out of these bitter raw materials Shakespeare fashions a demonstration of the necessity for mercy and love in so fallen a world, and a plot which avoids all physical misfortune while yet civilizing its characters with the most brutal of shock therapies. Both of the passionate male leads, Claudio and Angelo, see the misadventures of their love life become a topic of public discussion which leads to a death sentence for each. Here the eccentric symptoms of sexual desire have transcended their hitherto comic function in Shakespeare; instead of themes for purgative ridicule, these aberrations have now been transformed into near-tragic agents of "something of great constancy" in the final states of mind they bring about. Far more than Portia's simple assertions ever did, Isabella's role displays humanity's inescapable need for the higher Christian virtues of humility and mercy. While every character escapes ultimate penalties and even such confinement as Isabella's nunnery, it is only after meeting her challenge:

> Go to your bosom;
> Knock there, and ask your heart what it doth know
> That's like my brother's fault: if it confess
> A natural guiltiness such as is his,
> Let it not sound a thought upon your tongue
> Against my brother's life.   (II. ii. 136–141)

In such rueful recognitions there is no room for a spirit of romantic comedy, only for Dante's fuller "comic" resolution of human failures in the vision of his *Divine Comedy*.

Nevertheless, I think it is not accidental that *Measure for Measure* should be one of Shakespeare's most popular plays at present. Despite the distaste with which its sexual content has sometimes been greeted, its harsh humor and bawdy texture have always appealed to popular audiences. Nowadays, its explicit but provocative moral concerns seem particularly relevant—and not only with the resurgence of the venereal disease whose first onset from the Americas complicated sexual responses as much in Shakespeare's age as its renewed virulence has in our own. For we too are accustomed once more to discuss the ethical implications of the most intimate sexual actions with complete frankness in public. However, no "realistic" modern novel is any more explicit than this play about the destructive effects on personality of arbitrary sexual desire; and hardly any are capable of demonstrating these effects in such a comprehensive context of social, legal, and ethical considerations.

Moreover, the display of the inadequacies of sexual puritanism—either Angelo's repressiveness or Romeo's sentimentality—can serve as a Shakespearean figure for the destructive consequences of pursuing any rigid code too far, whether it be

Hotspur's cult of honor, Henry VI's saintly goal of a political society governed by love, or Richard III's absolute Machiavellianism. *Measure for Measure* shows that a character (whether Angelo or Isabella) who rates an idea higher than another's life will prove ultimately to be himself a pathological monstrosity incapable of sustaining even his own cherished ideological formula. Every principle in practice requires such infinite adjustment to assimilate all the details of each relevant occasion that every application proves to be a special case, so that skepticism about its applicability is the necessary prelude to successful enforcement of any law. This is the basis of the duke's relatively merciful if chastening sentence of marriage imposed on almost everyone in *Measure for Measure*. The play is a titillatingly particular series of illustrations of the truth which Shakespeare (at about the same period) causes Hamlet to uncover when he rejects Polonius's proposal to treat the actors "according to their desert": "God's bodykins, man, much better: use every man after his desert, and who should 'scape whipping? Use them after your own honour and dignity: the less they deserve, the more merit is in your bounty" (II. ii. 552–558). It has always been the defect of both political and moral extremes to pursue ideological absolutes with a righteous enthusiasm which is itself the negation of the highest morality and which, no less significantly, usually ends by defeating its own aims. Firmly married men are less likely to make this mistake, so the duke's reform of Vienna's sexual license through enforcement of matrimony should take care of future reformers too. Hasty idealism is unlikely to survive that experience, as we see in *Othello*.

DESDEMONA, AND CLEOPATRA'S ESCAPE
FROM TRAGIC VIRTUE

That stereotype of the Elizabethan gallant, Sir Philip Sidney, set a precedent in the sociology of modern literary criticism when he denounced the theater which was to produce Shakespeare. Sophisticated critics' views do often seem to correlate inversely with the taste of the intelligent general public of the time. Thus many disciples of D. H. Lawrence agree with F. R. Leavis, his most prominent British expositor, that the widely read *Lady Chatterley's Lover* is one of Lawrence's most feeble novels, full of phony characters, overformalized sex, and pompous language. By contrast, James Joyce's "obscene" *Ulysses* has been praised as "the greatest twentieth-century novel," but when it was reissued as a Penguin recently even enthusiastic reviewers like V. S. Pritchett and Philip Toynbee ruefully recognized that it has been rightly ignored by the reading public, like the rest of Joyce. This paradox of taste applies to Shakespeare also: critics generally agree that *King Lear* is Shakespeare's greatest play, but its flailing attack on conventional morals has never been really popular. The sexual fascination of the plays which I have been discussing, like *The Taming of the Shrew* and *Measure for Measure,* has not protected them from being bitterly attacked by scholars. Yet these and other plays little respected by critics (like *Henry VI* or *Henry VIII*) have usually been extremely successful on the stage.

 Othello falls into a middle ground. It has clearly appealed to every age, and yet has been condescendingly treated by some of the leading critics of each era, from Thomas Rymer in the seventeenth century to T. S. Eliot in our own. Many have concentrated on making awkward points: that the play's chronology is impossible; that indeed Desdemona has no occasion to commit the adultery of which she is held to be guilty. By this argument in turn Othello is shown to be even more grotesquely the dupe of Iago; and his exotic nature is also held to be the cause of his downfall. Contemporary racial problems have distorted our responses to *Othello,* as to Shylock in *The Merchant of Venice.* We project our own guilt over racial discrimination onto any earlier writer who dared to treat ethnic minorities as serious subjects in his discussion of human capacity (most modern geneticists and psychologists have wisely fled this area). Yet surely if a Jew or a Moor is shown to make misjudgments this does not prove the author is a racist. Indeed the dignity of their stories is enhanced in Shakespeare's case, where it can be shown that their "misjudgments" are really the result of tragic virtues, not of the author's crude moralism implicit in the pious concept of the "tragic flaw." Any work in which the hero really does seem to fail because of a "flaw" is necessarily shallow and false to our experience that "the rain falls on the just and the unjust."

The reason that *Othello* fascinates its audiences may well be precisely that its two principals are so genuinely impressive, and because of the plausible way in which their flamboyant downfall grows out of their own good intentions (as Iago says, II. iii. 367–368). *Othello* shows us in its most drastic and impressive form a truth uncovered by the *Sonnets*, that passionate relationships between individuals are dangerous in direct proportion to the sincerity and excellence of the lovers. It is the exclusion of the sardonic spirit of Iago from the relationship between Desdemona and Othello that insures their lack of precautions against him. This makes their love defenseless against malice from without, for which Iago is largely an arbitrary symbol. What destroys Othello is not the proneness to jealousy of that "African" temperament which was so crudely affected by Sir Laurence Olivier in a recent performance. Rather, it is Othello's commitment to virtue and firmness: his superiority to the limitations of Shakespeare's earlier romantic heroes makes his downfall a more emotionally profound experience for audiences.

Othello may ultimately choose to murder his wife rather than have intercourse with her, but he does so with deep if grotesque regret, and he does better than Hamlet at least in being able to bed his mistress effectively *before* his idealism stifles her vitality. *Othello* also portrays communities like Venice, where women are allowed a fuller scope. Even Gertrude might look less aberrant in Venice than she does in Elsinore. Moreover, however ironically for Othello, Cyprus is sacred to Aphrodite. It is surely such a healthy recognition of the physiological foundations of human survival which has given *Othello* its extraordinary claims on popular approval. The progression from the Vienna of *Measure for Measure* to the Venice of *Othello* is from the Waste Land which Reformation ethics often made of the Fallen World to the rich New World of the imagination legitimized by the Age of Discovery. Shakespeare's East affords him the same images of opulence and sensual satisfaction that the Americas suggested to More and Montaigne. Each sees in the geographical move away from Europe a liberation from the ethical restraints of merely conventional Christianity. And Venice is deeply tinctured by the exotic culture of its Levantine empire: even Desdemona's father Brabantio is deeply drawn to the exotic personality of the Moorish general.

Desdemona herself is unique in Shakespeare: she is a daughter of this new spirit of the Age of Discovery. Unlike all his other heroines, she transcends the conventional limits of archetypal female ambitions, either conventional (like the sexual and matrimonial ambitions of a Helena or a Katharina) or unorthodox (like the neurotic political ambitions of a Joan of Arc or a Lady Macbeth). Desdemona is enamored of Othello less as an individual than as an incarnation of the zeitgeist of an adventurous epoch. All too candidly, Othello confesses the purely mental appeal on which her love for him is founded in describing her response to his account of his life:

> My story being done,
> She gave me for my pains a world of sighs:
> She swore, in faith, 'twas strange, 'twas passing strange,
> 'Twas pitiful, 'twas wondrous pitiful:
> She wish'd she had not heard it, yet she wish'd
> That heaven had made her such a man: she thank'd me
> And bade me, if I had a friend that loved her,
> I should but teach him how to tell my story,
> And that would woo her. Upon this hint I spake:
> She loved me for the dangers I had pass'd.

> (I. iii. 158–167)

Contrasted with the physical diffidence and sexual indirectness of even such dashing comic heroines as Portia and Rosalind, the naked avowals of her ambitions put Desdemona in a very different category: she is the intellectual equivalent of the New Woman whom Shaw detected in the forthright sexual initiatives of Helena. It is precisely in this kind of superiority to the clichés of femininity that Desdemona's role moves the play beyond the scope of the *Sonnets* into the vision of a new toughness and intellectual authority. Indeed she sketches out the mentality of the frontierswoman who will domesticate the American wilderness:

> That I did love the Moor to live with him,
> My downright violence and storm of fortunes
> May trumpet to the world: my heart's subdued
> Even to the very quality of my lord:
> I saw Othello's visage in his mind,
> And to his honours and his valiant parts
> Did I my soul and fortunes consecrate,
> So that, dear lords, if I be left behind, . . .
> The rites for which I love him are bereft me.
>
> (I. iii. 249–256, 258)

It is another proof of the great virtue of Othello that he clearly accepts her adventurous spirit as the sole reason for her accompanying of him to Cyprus:

> I therefore beg it not
> To please the palate of my appetite,
> Nor to comply with heat—the young affects
> In me defunct—and proper satisfaction,
> But to be free and bounteous to her mind.
>
> (I. iii. 262–266)

The first act of *Othello* resonates to the Renaissance conviction of the dignity of human nature, and the play's extraordinary positive energies reveal not only why, historically, the Mohammedan threat to Europe was definitively smashed about this period but also why Europe was to dominate the rest of the world for the next three hundred and fifty years. In Desdemona we see a worthy figure for the boldness and discrimination of the European mind. In discrimination, she starts close to those new levels of awareness where the matured speaker of the *Sonnets* leaves off:

> In the old age black was not counted fair,
> Or if it were, it bore not beauty's name;
> But now is black beauty's successive heir.   (127)

Just as More saw in an American *Utopia* the opportunity for a critique of European values, or Montaigne could speak approvingly *Of Cannibals,* so Desdemona rejects her homeland and her father for new ideals of worth and conduct.

But *Othello* is a tragedy. It is so precisely because it largely lacks humor. And humor lies in a sense of the discrepancy between "official" personality and the arbitrary eccentricities enforced on human nature by chance and time,

> whose million'd accidents
> Creep in 'twixt vows and change decrees of kings,
> Tan sacred beauty, blunt the sharp'st intents,
> Divert strong minds to the course of altering things.
>
>   (115)

Even the play's wittiest character, Iago, is just as confident of the deliberateness of personality as the play's two principal characters. He asserts that " 'tis in ourselves that we are thus or thus. Our bodies are our gardens, to the which our wills are gardeners. . . . If the balance of our lives had not one scale of reason to poise another of sensuality, the blood and baseness of our natures would conduct us to most preposterous conclusions: but we have reason to cool our raging motions, our carnal stings, our unbitted lusts, whereof I take this that you call love to be a sect or scion" (I. iii. 333 ff).

The major difference between the views of Iago and Desde-

mona about human volition lies in their sense of its goals: Iago's
goals are always deliberately selfish, Desdemona's progressively
less so. Hers are never concealed; his are always masked, even
from himself. Unlike Desdemona, Iago makes one further step in
accepting the deliberateness of human choice: if we are fully
capable of self-definition, we are also capable of affecting false self-
definitions. In this awareness lies the source of all Iago's wit,
humor, and dominion over others. Neither Desdemona nor
Othello can allow for the inevitable discrepancies between base
reality and their ideal but artificial images of themselves or others.
In heroically committing themselves to viewing the optimum as
normal they have also unwittingly committed themselves to the
vigorous repudiation of anything less. They are perfectly correct
in regarding each other as worthy of the highest admiration, but
just because of this neither can conceive of even the appearance of
failure in the other. Not only can they not laugh at themselves or
at others' follies; they even find it impossible to laugh *with* others:

> I am not merry; but I do beguile
> The thing I am, by seeming otherwise.
>
> (II. i. 123–124)

Ironically only in repudiating even this trace of affected humor
does Desdemona for an instant display a hint of Iago's consciousness of the many levels of awareness which make up a full
personality.

For all her sense that Othello is not to be judged by his mere
appearance, she cannot master any of the other misrepresentations
that appearances will continue to provide. The contemptuous comment of the seventeenth-century neoclassical critic Thomas Rymer
that the play "may be a warning to all good Wives, that they look
well to their Linnen," is profoundly illuminating, however unintentionally. Just because visible personalities are artificial, personal
judgments about them are also superficial and the erratic com-
plexities of experience must be allowed for both in judging and in

controlling relationships. Desdemona always judges more flexibly than Othello, but she does not adequately sense that not only must an honorable life be lived, it must be seen to be lived. She pays too little attention to those niceties of display so dear to Iago's public persona. She does not mind nagging at her husband if it is in a good cause, and she heedlessly loses love tokens in the heat of emotional crises. Even so easily are false judgments fostered in others. Desdemona's great failure does indeed lie in losing the handkerchief and in not understanding why such a triviality is the most likely source of disasters. There is no skeptical Petruchio to teach her this. She also lacks Rosalind's wry sense of human frivolity.

    Othello displays a painful corollary of the strenuous energies which created the New World, the capacity for solemn idiocies as sinister as the Massachusetts witch trials. A strong and legitimate sense of virtue is often not merely fatal to one's sense of humor, but simply fatal. The contrast between *Othello* and *Antony and Cleopatra* may not be so great as is suggested by the latter's marked humorous elements. Each play presents the disastrous infatuation of a great general with a uniquely gifted woman, and both generals die as the result of a contemptible misunderstanding. Yet most of the one play is deeply tragic, while the other is scarcely ever melancholy despite moments of great bitterness. Indeed the curiously exhilarating tone of *Antony and Cleopatra* eludes traditional categories so completely that the mere lack of conventional terms of reference has largely contributed to its neglect.

    Nevertheless, this play more than any other shows us how Shakespeare's genius progressed beyond the tragic world of his "greatest" plays into the mature serenity of his last phase. And it is the full re-assimilation of the spirit of his sexual comedy into the world of "tragic virtues" which neutralizes the corrosive bitterness of the earlier tragic vision. It is precisely because Cleopatra can laugh at Antony and herself that she transforms her story from the lugubrious stereotype that Chaucer's Monk's Tale or Dryden's sentimental *All for Love* make of it, into a sparkling comedy which defies us to make of the play's conclusion more than an incident in a richly complex and vital whole. For this reason *Antony and Cleopatra* also represents the most ambitious ultimate phase of Shakespeare's sexual comedy: its integration into a world of the highest political import whose potentialities are nevertheless shown to be as erratic as those of our own—a world where there are not only quaint misunderstandings such as plague the heroes and heroines of the comedies but also the ever-present possibility that these will suddenly evolve into irreversible international disasters. In the "comic" environment of *Much Ado* we never believe that Hero will be allowed to die of shame, or that Benedick will finally have to kill Claudio for his cruelty. But in *Antony and Cleopatra* we laugh heartily in the very presence of deaths corroborated by history. When we contrast it with the collapse of Marlowe's worldly values into hopeless pessimism before the sustained recognition of death and damnation, both in *Tamburlaine* and in *Dr. Faustus,* this cheerful poise of Shakespeare at the climactic, fatal moments of *Antony and Cleopatra* becomes a supreme illustration of the resilience of the human spirit. The merriness is not simply an evasion but reflects a sense that life is too complex to be subsumed under a single category or mood, even when it is narrowed to the intense focus of an intended suicide. The unfashionableness of *Antony and Cleopatra* lies in its confident rejection of both aesthetic and psychological consistency. It is the supreme dramatic hybrid: at once comedy, tragedy, and history play.

It may even claim to verge on farce occasionally. For Cleopatra shares with St. Paul the capacity to be "all things to all men" —though no doubt for different motives. How alien to Marlowe's stiff ideal of the impact of Helen's classic beauty is this little retrospective vignette of Cleopatra's dominance of her lover:

> *Cleo.*   Give me mine angle; we'll to the river; there,
>   My music playing far off, I will betray
>   Tawny-finn'd fishes; my bended hook shall pierce

> Their slimy jaws; and, as I draw them up,
> I'll think them every one an Antony,
> And say 'Ah, ha! you're caught.'
> *Char.*   'Twas merry when
> You wager'd on your angling; when your diver
> Did hang a salt-fish on his hook, which he
> With fervency drew up.
> *Cleo.*   That time,—O times!—
> I laugh'd him out of patience; and that night
> I laugh'd him into patience; and next morn,
> Ere the ninth hour, I drunk him to his bed;
> Then put my tires and mantles on him, whilst
> I wore his sword Philippan.   (II. v. 10–23)

Like almost every part of the play, this passage has an extraordinary density of meaning. On one level it suggests an almost mystical range of personality. And it can as readily be understood in pagan as in Christian terms: Cleopatra obviously can successfully assume any role that she aspires to, and, in Terence's famous phrase, nothing human seems alien to her—even transvestism, "for vilest things / Become themselves in her" (II. ii. 243–244). But if she can tease Antony outrageously, she can also drink him under the table and usurp his virility openly, in a way far more disturbing than Rosalind's bisexuality or even Helena's relentless conquest of Bertram's will. Like St. Joan or the Duchess of Gloucester in *Henry VI,* or Lady Macbeth, Cleopatra carries an affectation of virility beyond instructive play to a sustained rejection of her biological role. Unlike Shakespeare's purely comic heroines, Cleopatra seriously aspires to military prowess, and the results are such disasters as Actium, which proves that her too aggressive reversal of sexual roles does indeed merit the censure of Enobarbus and "puzzle Antony; / Take from his heart, take from his brain" (III. vii. 11–12).

Far less offensive is her affectation of imperial dignity in the famous Cydnus performance, or even her assumption of the role of the Great Earth Mother when she enthrones herself and amidst her progeny, dressed "in the habiliments of the goddess Isis" (III. vi. 17). These are roles compatible with her status, sex, and temperament in a way that brandishing a sword in earnest is clearly not. However, it is in her range of comic roles that Cleopatra proves herself not merely sexually irresistible but as witty and imaginative as any of the heroines of the mature comedies. Enobarbus perfectly defines for us her power to dramatize situations memorably only a few moments before we see this faculty in action, when he says of Antony's impending departure: "Cleopatra, catching but the least word of this, dies instantly; I have seen her die twenty times upon far poorer moment" (I. ii. 145 ff). There is literal exactness in Antony's rueful rejoinder: "She is cunning past man's thought." Male reason cannot match Cleopatra's intuitive agility, and we at once see the deliberately paradoxical nature of her mind in her inquiries after Antony in the next scene:

> See where he is, who's with him, what he does:
> I did not send you: if you find him sad,
> Say I am dancing: if in mirth, report
> That I am sudden sick: quick, and return. (I. iii. 2–5)

Predictably, when he seeks to take his leave from Egypt, Antony is shot through by her reproaches, until he stands stupefied, like a Benedick riddled by the barbed witticism of a Beatrice who, in *Much Ado,* is shown "huddling jest upon jest with such impossible conveyance upon me that I stood like a man at mark, with a whole army shooting at me. She speaks poniards, and every word stabs" (II. i. 251 ff.).

But Cleopatra's range is far beyond that of Beatrice; it condescends to insult, but only as a foil to provocative visions of ecstasy:

> What says the married woman? You may go:
> Would she had never given you leave to come!

<pre>
        Let her not say 'tis I that keep you here:
        I have no power upon you; hers you are.
Ant.   The gods best know,—
Cleo.   O, never was there queen
        So mightily betray'd! yet at the first
        I saw the treasons planted.
Ant.   Cleopatra,—
Cleo.   Why should I think you can be mine and true,
        Though you in swearing shake the throned gods,
        Who have been false to Fulvia? Riotous madness,
        To be entangled with those mouth-made vows,
        Which break themselves in swearing!
Ant.   Most sweet queen,—
Cleo.   Nay, pray you, seek no colour for your going,
        But bid farewell, and go: when you sued staying,
        Then was the time for words: no going then;
        Eternity was in our lips and eyes,
        Bliss was in our brows' bent; none our parts so poor,
        But was a race of heaven: they are so still,
        Or thou, the greatest soldier of the world,
        Art turn'd the greatest liar.   (I. iii. 20–39)
</pre>

The issue is raised with all the insight of the ladies censuring the inconsistency of the fickle gallants in *Love's Labour's Lost*. But here there is a delicate blend of pathos, idealism, affected indignation, and calculated anticlimax which is beyond the rhetorical powers with which the youthful Shakespeare was able to invest the princess or her companions; and Beatrice could never rise to the lyrical conviction of phrases like "Eternity was in our lips and eyes," even if she *could* finish an elegant paragraph with as thunderous an exclamation as this one about the "greatest liar."

Cleopatra's endless costume changing is thus the surface evidence of her mastery of the art of role-playing in a purely psychological sense, a skill in which she excels any earlier Shakespearean character, even such spectacular ones as Richard III and Falstaff. For neither of these can attain her range and conviction. The essentially skeptical, villainous Richard never fully accepts the validity of his outer persona, and the grotesquely fat Falstaff can only hope to parody most serious attitudes since they necessarily conflict with his physical attributes and known actions. But Cleopatra slips into a role so completely that it ceases to be an affectation. Each new quirk of personality thus proves ultimately to be less a mere momentary performance than a permanent revelation of her potentialities which need not involve any rejection of earlier moods:

> I saw her once
> Hop forty paces through the public street;
> And having lost her breath, she spoke, and panted,
> That she did make defect perfection,
> And, breathless, power breathe forth.   (II. ii. 233–237)

Shakespeare has presented us with a figure whose power to grow exceeds that of any other of his creations. Compared to Rosalind or Isabella, Cleopatra shows a sense of the richness of human personality as superior to theirs as theirs are to the mechanical stereotypes of the doctrinaire psychologists of the twentieth century. Much more than Dryden's lively satiric portrait of the protean Buckingham in *Absalom and Achitophel's* Zimri, Cleopatra deserves being praised as a person "so various that she seems to be / Not one but all mankind's epitome." This flexibility sometimes produces astounding contrasts, such as her melodramatic treatment of the messenger who brings her news of Antony's marriage to Octavia:

> Hence,
> > *Strikes him again.*
> Horrible villain! or I'll spurn thine eyes
> Like balls before me; I'll unhair thy head:
> > *She hales him up and down.*
> Thou shalt be whipp'd with wire, and stew'd in brine,
> Smarting in lingering pickle.   (II. v. 62–66)

Only a few seconds later she defines her own failures in sober terms which seem incompatible with such behavior:

> These hands do lack nobility, that they strike
> A meaner than myself; since I myself
> Have given myself the cause.   (II. v. 82–84)

One sees at once that Cleopatra learns from her mistakes. Yet this never means she becomes a simple consistent person—for the scene ends on an erratic note about Antony:

> Let him for ever go:—let him not—Charmian,
> Though he be painted one way like a Gorgon,
> The other way he's Mars. Bid you Alexas
> Bring me word how tall she is. Pity me, Charmian,
> But do not speak to me.   (II. v. 115–119)

However, like Antony, Cleopatra would rather keep all her options open than maintain an honorable consistency. If Antony seemingly betrays Cleopatra in sealing an alliance with Caesar by his marriage to Caesar's sister Octavia, Cleopatra equally entertains the possibility of switching from her lover to Caesar, only to be caught by Antony entertaining the enemy agent. Antony's abuse of her is no less justified than was Enobarbus's praise of her; even to the end of the play, when she tries to conceal her jewelry from Caesar, Cleopatra merits Antony's judgment that "You have been a boggler ever" (III. xiii. 110).

It is precisely her capacity to visualize the fullest range of possible behavior, from the best to the worst, which makes Cleopatra so fascinating a figure. She is committed narrowly neither to impossible and fatal standards of perfection like Desdemona or Cordelia nor to relentless villainy like Queen Margaret or Lady Macbeth. At any instant her choices are totally open, and the duration and complexity of her life suggests that whatever their local limitations, her performance has been substantially well-

guided. Only the Machiavellian finesse of Octavius proves beyond
the mastery of her temperament, just as Falstaff ultimately meets
his doom at the hands of King Henry V, whose subtlety he had
himself fostered when he was Prince Hal. But the defeat of
Cleopatra is not a pathetic one like the casting off of Falstaff. She
loses all of her characteristic comic options, but in the choice of
suicide she shows a last and most dazzling authority over circumstance:

> I shall show the cinders of my spirits
> Through the ashes of my chance.   (V. ii. 173–174)

Though the last four long scenes of the play have no trace of
sexual comedy, they still display to perfection the quality of mind
produced by the tempering experience of complex and sustained
sexual relationships. There is no attempt to disguise their inescapable sexual folly, though Antony's suicide is less the simple
result of Cleopatra's resort once again to the pretense of suicide
than of the weary recognition that his defeat by Caesar is inevitable. That Antony accepts his fate as barely premature if he is
to salvage any dignity appears in his total acceptance of his impending death even when he discovers that Cleopatra is, as usual,
still alive. The sentimental extravagance which alone killed Romeo
merely provides a picturesque occasion for Antony's self-destruction, an act which depends primarily on the need to meet his
defeat in high Roman fashion:

> The miserable change now at my end
> Lament nor sorrow at; but please your thoughts
> In feeding them with those my former fortunes
> Wherein I lived, the greatest prince o' the world,
> The noblest; and do now not basely die,
> Not cowardly put off my helmet to
> My countryman,—a Roman by a Roman
> Valiantly vanquished.   (IV. xv. 51–58)

Moreover, if Antony wounds himself thinking his mistress dead, and in a mood of romantic melancholy, he does so without holding her immediate betrayals against her once he judges her in the light of eternity. She may on occasion have deserved the charge of being a "triple-turn'd whore" (IV. xii. 14) but he finds her failures do not ultimately deserve such censure: "I will o'ertake thee, Cleopatra, and / Weep for my pardon" (IV. xiv. 44–45). Even more strikingly, having discovered her final fatal misrepresentation, he also finds any comment on it quite unnecessary. Like the experienced lover of the Dark Lady, he finds that overt recognition of his mistress' dishonesties seems superfluous to him; he accepts his death and is exclusively concerned with last-minute practical advice: "Gentle, hear me: / None about Caesar trust but Proculeius" (IV. xv. 47–48). Nothing could better illustrate the resigned good sense of the mature lover, making the best of the follies he shares with his fallible beloved. Like the dying Desdemona, Antony is concerned only to help his beloved survive, even though she seems mistakenly to have brought about his own death.

This positive response to the failure of one's lover is the state of mind at which Shakespeare aims the developing awareness of all the "victims" in his sexual comedies; and we may well conclude this survey by wondering how far Cleopatra shares it with Antony. It is customary for critics to observe that by her resolution to kill herself Cleopatra shows that she has learnt something of Antony's Roman dignity and that this redeems her earlier frivolity. However, the superficial cause of Antony's bungled suicide appears to be his sentimental response to the misreport of Cleopatra's death, an erratic mental condition deftly reinforced by Shakespeare's stress on the name of his attendant in this highly emotional scene: Eros. Similarly, Cleopatra's suicidal feelings are nominally governed by the vision of an unearthly relationship with Antony, even though she also sees the dignity of self-destruction in comparison with the humiliations of being Caesar's captive. Her death is not actually achieved "after the high Roman fashion" (IV. xv. 87) any more than Antony's has been. His was handled as awkwardly as the belly-shattering suicide of Lövborg in *Hedda Gabbler,* while the dignity of Cleopatra's death is subtly tainted by the ridicule and grotesqueness of its context: her lying to conceal her jewelry, the wry comments of the Clown who brings the asps, the repellent mode of her suicide, and even such minor details as her last pose in death ("Your crown's awry" V. ii. 321). There is also surely a strong negative association intended when Cleopatra kisses Iras and the attendant drops dead on the spot.

Despite uniform opinion in favor of her "reform," Cleopatra at the end of the play is scarcely a Roman matron. Even if she does call Antony "husband," she is no Octavia. The supreme virtue of Cleopatra's state of mind at the end of the play is simpler and more pathetic than an improbable transformation into a Lucrece; it lies in her admission of her simple dependence on her beloved:

> No more, but e'en a woman, and commanded
> By such poor passion as the maid that milks
> And does the meanest chores.   (IV. xv. 73–75)

Such humble acceptance of her sexual dependence on Antony requires a complete revision of our attitude to Cleopatra's previous displays of versatility in sexual role-playing. The most important feature of her virtuosity now proves to lie in its least obvious feature: that it coexists with a genuine passion which is not the less intense for being avowed only involuntarily in moments of stress, or in a little parenthesis like the one in which she mentions Antony's horse: "O happy horse, to bear the weight of Antony!" (I. v. 21). Shakespeare seems to feel that Cleopatra's supreme virtue as a lover lies in her capacity to enjoy her sexuality intensely yet never to allow these feelings to overthrow her self-command in the presence of her beloved. She illustrates in this the same strength as Beatrice and Rosalind, both of whom normally also maintain their witty poise in the presence of men to whom they are violently attracted. Admiration of the power to feel deeply and yet to act and speak wittily is the end product of Shakespeare's study of sexual relations. It is this comic faculty which is lacking in the sexual relations of Desdemona and Othello, and even in Antony—who cannot always comprehend that the provocative surface of Cleopatra's personality need not be incompatible with a deep attachment and loyalty to him. In the midst of one of his more intense denunciations of her untrustworthiness and frivolity, she murmurs sadly, "Not know me yet?" (III. xiii. 157).

The conclusion we must draw from this broad survey of Shakespeare's exposition of sexual relationships is thus profoundly disconcerting. It suggests that his great love scenes are not those enshrined by conventional critical judgment, where sentimental passion finds outlet only in frantic rhetoric and flamboyant imagery. As between Romeo's aureate fluency and Juliet's faintly satirical rejoinders, the proof of maturity lies with the latter. Othello's outspoken vehemence is a symptom of his sexual inexperience, not of the depth and richness of his feeling for Desdemona. By contrast, Portia's teasing of Bassanio or Helena's firm manipulation of her husband's promiscuity displays the admirable discrimination governing their feelings for lovers whose physical necessity to them is nevertheless covertly recognized in numerous admissions by the women. The "great" lovers in Shakespeare—Romeo, Troilus, Othello, and Antony—are all guilty of failures which are in part surely intended to admonish us against their mistakes. The truly successful lovers are those whose response to sexuality always seeks to divert commitment back from its tragic potentiality, toward comedy: a Petruchio or a Benedick, a Portia or a Cleopatra. Perhaps only in Shakespeare can we find a fully conscious exposition of that paradoxical coexistence of discrimination and commitment of which Eliot saw traces in Donne, and which Donne may well have learned from Shakespeare in the first place:

> When my love swears that she is made of truth
> I do believe her, though I know she lies, ...

Greatness of mind lies in this capacity to confront mutually exclusive truths without loss of poise. An immature personality like Troilus cannot do this when faced with the fickleness of his beloved:

> If there be rule in unity itself,
> This is not she. O madness of discourse,
> That cause sets up with and against itself!
> Bi-fold authority! where reason can revolt
> Without perdition, and loss assume all reason
> Without revolt: this is, and is not, Cressid.
>
> (V. ii. 141–146)

It is the proof of Benedick's contrasting maturity and stability that he can continue to act even when he becomes totally ridiculous from a "reasonable" point of view by marrying a woman who affects not to love him, against his own previous pronouncements: "I'll tell thee what, prince; a college of witcrackers cannot flout me out of my humour. Dost thou think I care for a satire or an epigram? No: if a man will be beaten with brains, a' shall wear nothing handsome about him. In brief, since I do purpose to marry, I will think nothing to any purpose that the world can say against it; and therefore never flout at me for what I have said against it; for man is a giddy thing, and this is my conclusion" (V. iv. 101 ff). The only successful and even faintly dignified lover here appears to be the one who accepts the inevitability of his own ludicrousness in the light of the limitations of his beloved, and takes steps to cope with it. Any sanctification of intense sexuality as a good in itself will serve merely to heighten the lover's grotesqueness, potentially to the point of disaster. For Shakespeare, there is not a distinction between a comic kind of love and a serious kind; true love survives only by a sense of the comedy of sex. There is no substantial alternative.

CHAPTER FIVE

Shakespeare and Modern Sexuality: Albee's "Virginia Woolf" and "Much Ado"

B RINGING facts about the private life of an author into formal discussion of his work is usually considered tactless. Yet few fictions can be so fully grasped by themselves that a sense of their autobiographical contexts will not clarify the works' scope and limitations. Tactfully handled, the *argumentum ad hominem* often adds at least comedy and even excitement to one's reading of any text, however dull. And while a work of real distinction will always transcend a mere analysis of its author's life, its insights must necessarily rise out of what was first a specifically personal illumination attained by the writer under a particular set of circumstances. Nothing seems to me more fraudulent in writing than to affect complete impartiality, objectivity, and comprehensiveness. The human mind is not and can never be omniscient. The suppression of one's individual perspective in any argument is not merely a falsification of the origins of the evidence comparable to the myth of "scientific method." Affected objectivity also allows a greater tyranny of judgment over others than when views are tempered by an avowal of one's personal interest in the issue. That is why anonymity is the mark of intellectual pretentiousness, if it is not the symptom of conflict of interest. It is also why I have rejected the conventional objective style in the present book. My comments are based on many years of careful thought and observation, but they are also the result of the interaction of the material with my own private experience. If we deny ourselves the recognition of the bearing of such experience on any intellectual activity, however elevated, we lose important clues to understanding. The idea that any critic can fully master the content of a complex work of art without any external clues is a myth which could only be entertained by critical solipsists.

One of the characteristics of the Cambridge University School of English, where I earned my B.A., is that it stresses the continuing function of literature in society, which in turn implies the need to understand how it rises from that society. Shakespeare's plays are not purely aesthetic experiences for the English as they necessarily are for Californians. The plays continue in England to derive some of their impact from resources of immediacy which seem to me to be a necessary part of all meaningful art. At the crudest level, when Hotspur mentions Burton-on-Trent my mind necessarily reacts, because I was born in that ancient town, whose breweries date back to the medieval monks of a thousand years ago, and whose refounded abbey school first introduced me to the works of Shakespeare. Hardly a name in Shakespeare's histories lacks some such resonance for Englishmen. On a higher level, the moral and political issues of English government as they appear to a Midland poet born and bred in Warwickshire must harmonize to some extent even with those of a modern writer from the provinces like myself, if he was raised a few miles away from Stratford, in Staffordshire. When Shakespeare ridicules clever young graduates I am immediately reminded of my own contemporaries, some of whom are now beginning to run England in the spirit of the King of Navarre or Henry VI.

However, Edward Albee's smart young American professor in *Who's Afraid of Virginia Woolf?* is not simply the same kind of Renaissance intellectual as Lucentio or Biron. To suppose that would be to make the kind of mistake about Western continuity that some of my students make when they observe that anyone coming from East of the Sierras must uniformly look, sound, and behave in a characteristically archaic way which all those unfortunate people have who were raised anywhere east of the Sierra Nevada (and west of the Urals). What we have in Nick is the confident and ambitious "all-American" boy that Willy Loman so much admired, and this is something quite different from the nervous British graduate who succeeds Shakespeare's young wits as Kingsley Amis's hero in *Lucky Jim*. However, Nick does illustrate the same ratio between the immature yet gifted individual and his environment that we have seen in figures like Romeo, Bertram, and Claudio, as well as Jim Dixon. These figures share with Nick what his aging host, George, finds to be "the most profound indication of social malignancy . . . no sense of humor." They all take themselves and their goals too seriously. This similarity and the other analogies of structure, characterization, and texture between *Virginia Woolf* and Shakespeare's *Much Ado About Nothing* show that this analysis of Shakespearean comedy bears directly on the best expression of contemporary American experience and behavior.

It is not accidental that George, the most incisive figure in Albee's play, should be a professor of history. The play reflects Albee's own sense of the importance of a man's intellectual life taking place in the context of a tradition. This awareness in a superlatively successful play suggests how necessary it is for creative minds to seek the understanding of the present through comparison and contrast with the past. Unlike the plays of Miller and Williams, Albee's comedy is full of calculated echoes of Goethe, Shakespeare, and other figures prominent in the European tradition; but Albee never capitulates to that tradition as did some authors in the older generations of American writers. He is no slave to Shakespeare, and the explicit evidence of his knowledge of this prototype is of an incidental kind. He clearly intends us to recognize that the household of George and Martha is to be a scene of emotional purification comparable to those achieved in Shake-

spearean settings like the Forest of Arden or Lear's stormy heath.
Northrop Frye has characterized such places as "the Green World,"
in which Shakespeare's characters discover a deeper, more spontaneous psychic reality than they ever do in routine urban life. But
such a purgative setting need not be a rural landscape. It can be
any unfamiliar locale: the elusive seacoast of Bohemia, for example,
or even a gathering transfigured by alcohol and held at 3 A.M. in
the home of a history professor. Albee understands Shakespeare's
technique of therapeutic displacement and makes George welcome
his naive and unsuspecting guests by suggesting they have arrived
in the land of Shakespeare's *Twelfth Night:* "And this . . . *(With
a handsweep taking in not only the room, the house, but the whole
countryside)* . . . this is your heart's content—Illyria." *Twelfth
Night* is a play whose plot serves as a gallery for victims of quaint
sexual neuroses. It has remained amusing enough to this day to
have been transformed into a modern popular smash-hit in New
York and San Francisco as a musical comedy, *Your Own Thing.*
Obviously, Albee knows he is wittily recreating the same salutary
permutations of sexual unbalance that Shakespeare achieved in
Illyria.

Like all Shakespeare's sexual comedy, Albee's is also founded
on a dictum which he attributes to George, about "All truth being
relative." Quaintly enough, Albee demonstrates this fact by using
the same kind of illustration as Petruchio used for Kate (and
which Shakespeare made the occasion of Romeo's first real disagreement with Juliet). Just after a somewhat abortive attempt at
adultery with young Nick, George's aging wife Martha is offered
some flowers by her husband, who claims he "went out into the
moonlight to pick 'em for Martha tonight." Martha flatly disagrees
with his observations: "There is no moon now. I saw it go down
from the bedroom." She and George then go into a vigorous argument about whether there was a moon or not, which clearly relates
ultimately to whether or not the intended adultery in that bedroom was actually consummated. George wins the argument by

asserting "the moon may very well have gone down . . . but it came back up." To Martha's astounded incredulity he proves that this is possible, since it all depends on the point of view of the observer. He explains that to a traveler the moon may seem to set behind a mountain, only to reappear when the obstruction is left behind by the motion of the car or ship. Similarly Martha may feel that Nick's incapacity to complete the sexual act frees her from the charge of any actual adultery; but George understandably intends to stress that for him the intent is quite sufficient to prove guilt. He is placed in Helena's state of mind when Bertram thinks he is committing adultery with his new mistress: the fact that he is only making love to his wife Helena herself is not really so consoling to her in view of his intent to betray her.

Like most of Shakespeare's comedy, the heart of Albee's lies in such witty discussions that clarify subjective responses, and not in any action or outcome which changes formal relationships. *Virginia Woolf* does not end with any rearrangement of partners. And just as in *Measure for Measure* Shakespeare often "cleans up" his sources by getting rid of their more brutal acts like rape and murder, so Albee insures that the attempted act of adultery in his play is frustrated by Nick's temporary impotence, induced superficially by alcohol ("Him can't. Him too fulla booze"). However, we are surely intended to assume that this failure is also significantly affected by the ultimate commitment to their marriages shown by everyone involved. For a modern author Albee shows an extraordinary concern to preserve ultimate values and avoid an irreversible showdown. As with the supposed death of Claudio's beloved Hero in *Much Ado*, Albee favors the cathartic appearance of horror, not its real occurrence. Martha only seems to commit adultery, for which she has in fact already been punished in anticipation when George whipped out his shotgun and fired at her. Of course it is appropriately a toy gun, from which "blossoms a large red and yellow Chinese parasol." The play abounds in such deflating effects. Indeed much of the interplay between George and Martha has the effect of a game sublimating potentially deadly instincts into therapeutically "violent" dialogue.

In these terms the function of the allusions to Virginia Woolf in the play cannot be underestimated. This authoress was the daughter of the famous Victorian man of letters Leslie Stephen, and her novels are based on intense subjectivity of the most delicate kind. Unfortunately this refined temperament frequently made life seem quite unbearable to her, and after making several attempts at suicide she was finally successful in 1941. For Albee the terrors of this temperamental Woolf are the civilized man's equivalent of the primitive fears enshrined in the nursery rhyme's "big bad wolf." Albee asks us to consider how modern man can exorcise the horrors of existence without forfeiting his civilized discriminations. His answer here is identical to Shakespeare's: to transfigure monstrosity with wit. This is not an evasion; Freud himself recognized jokes and laughter as devices for coming to terms with what we fear. And this pattern explains the duality of Albee's impact in this play. The defeated minds of certain modern American intellectuals welcome it because the play seems to show life to be as horrible as it appears to their own quivering sensibilities and those of a Virginia Woolf. With cries of masochistic joy they greet the play as "shattering," "excoriating," "terrifying" (I quote from the blurbs of the paperback edition). Of course, we know that no play attains permanent status on this basis. At the first New York production of this one, it was clear that while the audience was sometimes startled by the frankness of the dialogue, what really gripped them was the liveliness of the humor and the play's rewarding insights into sexual psychology. Far from being shocked, the audience greeted each sharp stroke of repartee with delighted laughter. That this play should also be one that sidestepped none of the harshest aspects of its theme was surely its moral virtue. That it should transmute this potentially distressing material into something creative and delightful is what really suggests its greatness. Unless we are masochists, we do not go to the theater or read novels merely to be told how horrible life can be; if we are not irredeemably insensitive we should know that already. As Aristotle said, we go to the theater to purge ourselves of excessive fear and debilitating sentimentality. *Virginia Woolf* is not fashionably disgusting, as some of the "best" critics would have it, but exhilarating and ultimately quite inoffensive and sane.

That all this is known to Albee is readily demonstrable from the text. In Shakespeare, the author's recognition of the therapeutic play of wit is visible in the characters' open comments: "Well bandied both; a set of wit well play'd," says the princess to her ladies after a bawdy exchange in *Love's Labour's Lost* (V. ii. 29). Cleopatra proudly describes Antony's fortunate susceptibility to her humor: "I laugh'd him into patience" (II. v. 20); and Enobarbus confirms the dominion of her vitality: "the holy priests / Bless her when she is riggish" (II. ii. 244–245). Albee's characters also recognize their virtuosity. After a verbal duel between George and Martha in which George claims they "are merely . . . exercising," Nick observes "Oh, you two don't miss . . . you two are pretty good. Impressive." After George successfully takes his revenge on Nick for his philandering with Martha by playing "a little game of Get the Guests," Martha comments expertly on his "pigmy hunting": "Very good, George. . . . really good." Reviewing her compulsive attachment to George after Nick's failure, Martha praises her husband because he "keeps learning the games we play as quickly as I can change the rules." As the princess says, "Good wits will be jangling" (II. i. 225); and in *Much Ado* Benedick finally observes to Beatrice: "Thou and I are too wise to woo peaceably" (V. ii. 75).

It is easy to show the antiquity of this kind of mutual abuse which is so cleverly damaging that it becomes funny as well as therapeutic. It has also long been understood that insult often implies a deep-rooted affection just because it is so extravagant. In *All's Well* an astounded bystander says of Parolles's slander of his patron Bertram: "He hath out-villained villainy so far that the rarity redeems him" (IV. iii. 305–306). Hal and Falstaff say the most unforgivable things to each other in the best of humor; yet when Hal quietly rejects Falstaff at the end of *Henry IV*, Falstaff is said to die of a broken heart. Indeed so conventional is the idea of ritual abuse between true friends that in medieval England it attained the status of a genre, the so-called "flyting." Thus the extreme insults that fly between George and Martha can reflect a deep love; they usually end in uproarious laughter and even sentimentality: "C'mon over here and give your Mommy a big sloppy kiss." However, let there be no doubt about it, their insults can be damaging and painful: "I swear," says Martha, "if you existed I'd divorce you." To which George later replies: "try to keep your clothes on, too. There aren't many more sickening sights than you with a couple of drinks in you and your skirt up over your head, you know." Sometimes George may be merely comically hyperbolic: "our son . . . the apple of our three eyes, Martha being a Cyclops." However, we should remember that the issues are not usually so frivolous: real tensions are being effectively worked off in the exchanges, as Albee stresses by having George physically attack Martha at one point when she mishandles the therapeutic technique.

The single lapse does not mean the technique is basically inadequate. Indeed modern psychiatrists are beginning positively to advocate it. From the point of view of the psychiatrist, the vicious verbal battles between George and Martha are not tragic proofs of failure but vindications of their vitality and the solidity of their marriage. By contrast, the conventional coldness of Nick and his spouse indicates a failed relationship: he admits he cannot make love to her successfully, and he also significantly fails with Martha. Albee is not the first writer to have had this insight. In the time of Julius Caesar, the Latin poet Catullus (born in Verona, no less) wrote of Clodia, the wife of an influential Roman:

> Lesbia for ever on me rails
> To talk of me she never fails.

> Now, hang me, but for all her art,
> I find that I have gained her heart.
> My proof is this: I plainly see
> The case is just the same with me;
> I curse her every hour sincerely,
> Yet, hang me, but I love her dearly.

Although Catullus understands that surface hostility often marks basic attraction, he does not display the full pattern shown in *Virginia Woolf;* to find a more comprehensive prototype we need to move to *Much Ado.* The battle between Benedick and Beatrice is as verbally violent as any in Shakespeare's comedy, yet it significantly avoids the physical exchanges of Petruchio and Katharina, ending in so complete an acceptance of marriage by the hero that his name has become a synonym for the "married man." No better testimony could be found for the play's authority than its hero's apotheosis into popular mythology.

Benedick and Beatrice are first shown to us at complete loggerheads. He greets her with "What, my dear Lady Disdain! are you yet living?" (I. i. 119). However, even before he enters she has scarcely disguised her interest in his arrival, for all their "merry war." Clearly there is something deeper concealed by the fact that "they never meet but there's a skirmish of wit between them" (I. i. 63). A minute scrutiny of the text suggests a few subliminal touches by Shakespeare which are intended to make us sense that Beatrice has already had an abortive affair with her "enemy." She observes to him that "you always end with a jade's trick: I know you of old" (I. i. 145). Later when told she has lost the heart of Benedick she sharply ripostes, "Indeed, my lord, he lent it me awhile; and I gave him use for it, a double heart for his single one; marry, once before he won it of me with false dice" (II. i. 285–290). The implication is that he once gave her his own dishonest love in exchange for her innocent one, so that her present trickiness is simply paying him back in kind. Ironically, the discipline of a love affair tempered in such mutual acrimony proves the best prelude to matrimony. Their friends are convinced that "She were an excellent wife for Benedick" (II. i. 366). The two have no illusions about each other, yet they are still attracted, as even Benedick concedes: "an she were not possessed with a fury, her cousin [Beatrice] exceeds [Hero] as much in beauty as the first of May doth the last of December" (I. i. 192–195).

The very violence of their surface antipathy thus validates the lovers' prompt surrender to affection when each is convinced by their friends of the other's commitment: "Love me! why, it must be requited," exclaims Benedick (II. iii. 230), only one scene after saying, "I would to God some scholar would conjure her; for certainly, while she is here, a man may live as quiet in hell as in a sanctuary; and people sin upon purpose, because they would go thither; so, indeed, all disquiet, horror and perturbation follows her" (II. i. 264–269). Similarly, after having just insulted Benedick "past the endurance of a block," Beatrice proves equally quick to reverse her judgment: "If thou dost love, my kindness shall incite thee" (III. i. 113). In such plausible yet violent oscillations we have the full precedent for Albee's startling alternations of mood in George and Martha. Shakespeare provides a classic precedent for the idea that virulence between man and woman is a function not of antipathy but of sympathy. Only people truly in love can endure such bitterness without committing some crime as dreadful as Claudio's repudiation of his bride at the very altar where they are about to be married, or Othello's murder of Desdemona.

Both Shakespeare and Albee deliberately stress the relative success of the sexual relationship between their harshly mature couples by using the inadequacies of their younger, more naive pairs of lovers as foils. Though Benedick may have affronted Beatrice in some suggested past, *Much Ado* is very careful to show how well he responds in the play itself to a challenge no less insidious than that before which his young friend Claudio fails. Precisely because Benedick has endured the worst that Beatrice can inflict, he cannot be shocked out of his resolved affection for her, even when she requires as proof of his trust in her that he "kill Claudio" (IV. i. 291), his best friend. That he reluctantly but unequivocally accepts the validity of his mistress' judgment of Claudio's failure suggests the extent to which a lover must risk trusting his beloved, even when he knows that she can be a shrew.

The irony is that the occasion for this proof of trust between two skeptics is precisely the collapse of trust between two pure and innocent lovers, who totally fail to cope with a false challenge to their devotion. Claudio adores Hero in a naively passionate way but proves capable of believing endless misrepresentations of her conduct, which she is not tough enough to refute. After learning his mistakes he has to concede his own inadequacy publicly by accepting a new, unseen bride (actually his old one in disguise), who is presented to him, not chosen by him. And Hero has to accept graciously a husband whom she knows to have shown the callowness of her once romantic but now dishonored suitor. Claudio and Hero are thus successfully married only after attaining a rueful awareness of their limitations not unlike that of Beatrice and Benedick at the start of the play. When it is finally proved that, unlike Hero and Claudio, the older lovers never did admit their affections for each other as their friends pretended, both are resilient and positive enough to overcome even this seemingly insuperable obstacle to their relationship. Their marriage depends on no naive positives: they know each other's faults to the full and they do not even have the compensations of violent desire. Precisely because they get married on the basis of an affection that is "no more than reason," a mere "friendly recompense" (V. iv. 71, 83), we are encouraged to believe that their marriage may be tempestuous yet will survive, unlike those of Romeo and Othello which start so euphorically.

One of the reasons that the parts of Beatrice and Benedick are so sought after by leading actors is that this is one of the few relationships in Shakespeare in which both lovers are witty, worldly-wise, and unwilling to let their passions dominate them.

The result is exhilarating in the theater. Many critics, focusing their attention on the grotesque misfortunes of the young romantic lead, think that the play is simply a botched melodrama. However, Claudio's incompetence is most valuable to the play simply as the occasion on which Benedick's love of Beatrice is tested and vindicated. Claudio's failure to handle the tricks of a stagey villain make it difficult to take him very seriously.

Despite its relatively low critical reputation, the play's wit and realism have favored its stage success. Its lively prose called out Gielgud's best Shakespearean performance opposite Peggy Ashcroft as Beatrice some years ago, in a production so brilliant that it was frequently revived. The naturalism of the dialogue appeals strongly to its audiences, as it plainly did in a recent production by the British National Theatre in San Francisco. Nevertheless, the play does have a flaw: the device by which Beatrice and Benedick are brought together is too contrived. It is true that they convincingly overcome this diminution of their powers of self-determination by reaffirming their love after being told of the deception, but they have been shown not to be fully autonomous individuals. This reduces their stature as mature lovers, just as the failure to "explain" the genesis of the wit and insight of figures like Biron and Petruchio diminishes their relevance to our own experience.

Shakespeare is not perfect, and it is useful to remind ourselves that he is not. The greatest failing of literary criticism is its habit of trying to overpower its readers with the grandeur of its subject. The supposedly miraculous superiority of Shakespeare's work may even explain the popularity of the ridiculous Baconian heresy (which is refuted by the unshakable testimony of Ben Jonson, not to mention Heminge and Condell). People are oppressed by the endless emphasis on Shakespeare's towering genius and get their revenge by challenging his claim to his own achievements. Bacon is a useful alternative because, for all his intellectual eminence, he contrasts with Shakespeare in having been such an unlovable man: disloyal to his patron, contemptuous of love and friendship, and ultimately dismissed from his post as chancellor for bribery—there is no risk of oppressive superiority in such a career.

Shakespeare was the first writer in English to create plausible presentations of the most complex and valuable types of sexual relationships. How definitively he did it is another matter: he had to depend on the Renaissance theater's weird jumble of only partially relevant literary conventions. Often this material needed radical readjustment to suit his ends, and some of the criticism leveled at him results from the difficulty of successfully adapting available plots to new purposes, as with *All's Well, Measure for Measure,* and *Much Ado.*

This criticism is often unfair, because it fails to recognize Shakespeare's novel intentions and insights. However, like all initiators, Shakespeare in no sense exhausts the possibilities of his own insights. In particular, the full autonomy of the characters of Beatrice and Benedick is realized only by later dramatists. One pair of theatrical lovers who are fully and plausibly self-determining is Congreve's Mirabel and Millamant. They are relentlessly self-disciplined on the surface, though totally committed at heart. Millamant ridicules the affectations of passion by using the reams of poetry devoted to her by lovers as curl papers. She makes a formal peace treaty with her lover as if marriage were an armed truce, even though she confesses to an acquaintance that she "loves him violently"—just as Rosalind confesses to Celia, "O coz . . . that thou didst know how many fathoms deep I am in love!" (IV. i. 212–213). Mirabel agrees that all the mannerisms of passion shall be renounced. Unlike those who affect to be in love but love chiefly its egotistical satisfactions, these worldly-wise lovers will preserve absolute social decorum. Being truly in love, they know how terrifyingly destructive their passion can be. They accept its basic imperative, despite the loss of that treasured sexual freedom implicit in their names: Mirabel ("admirer of beauty") and Millamant ("thousand lovers"). However, they will not allow it to destroy the civilized texture of their human relations: witty insults and rhetorical quarrels, yes; but no picturesque displays, such as murder or protests of eternal devotion.

The romantic notion that only physical violence proves sincerity seems at first sight to be supported by *Virginia Woolf,* since after all George does try (ineffectually) to beat Martha up, and intellectuals can therefore admire him for "caring." But this hint of tragic folly is important only as a foil to George's extraordinary good sense; it is a lapse which makes him plausible and human, but is not representative of a figure who is even spared participation in the holocaust of World War II. In fact, George is shown to be superior in plausibility to Shakespeare's best comic heroes, even though his distinction can best be grasped if we approach him through Shakespeare. Unlike Petruchio or Biron, George is no verbal superman invested with the full powers of a Shakespeare. He is an intelligent, well-informed, and competent man without special gifts, a perfect model for Everyman, if he proves worthy. And in an oblique way Albee builds him up considerably: he has been chairman of his department (though during the war); he has written a novel (though forbidden to publish it by his college); he is physically fit (though no match for a middle-weight champion). He knows the dangerous power of the ideal when he confronts Nick, whom he recognizes at once as his superior in every quality except the most important, human flexibility. George is immeasurably Nick's superior only if man's unique distinction is his adaptability (as zoologists tell us it is); but this is a virtue which always seems like a limitation in comparison with the local efficiency of the specialized organism headed for extinction after a blaze of temporary glory, like tyrannosaurus rex.

By comparison with George, Nick is a uniquely refined animal, perfected for success in the academic jungle: "What I thought I'd do is . . . I'd sort of insinuate myself generally, play around for a while, find all the weak spots, shore 'em up, but with my own name plate on 'em . . . become sort of a fact, and then turn into a . . . a what . . . ? Exactly. . . . An inevitability. You know. . . . Take over a few courses from the older men, start some special groups for myself . . . plow a few pertinent wives. . . ." Such men are in no sense unusual or insignificant. George catches the quality of selective genius in Nick: he sees that here is a mind which might impose its systems on society in the interests of apparent perfection: "All imbalances will be corrected, sifted out . . . propensity for various diseases will be gone, longevity assured. We will have a race of men . . . test-tube-bred . . . incubator-born . . . superb and sublime." It is a vision of order shared by such Shakespearean intellectuals as Longaville, before they fall into disillusion.

George's critique is that of the generalist who sees the fatal inflexibility of such a narrow vision, its incompatibility with life in all "its glorious variety and unpredictability." He senses that in the world he knows what is important is not systems but adaptability. Mutability requires mutation, and George is positively chameleon-like in his role-switching, which is why Martha can truthfully say to him, "if you existed I'd divorce you," and tell others that "he wasn't particularly . . . aggressive," and "he didn't have any personality." George is like Shakespeare's persona in the *Sonnets:* he cannot be rejected by his lover, because he is too agile to give her grounds for enduring resentment. Albee is clever enough to synthesize for Martha the point of view which must have been that of Shakespeare's overpowered Dark Lady and his friend, when she speaks of "George who is good to me, and whom I revile; who understands me, and whom I push off; who can make me laugh, and I choke it back in my throat; who can hold me at night, so that it's warm, and whom I will bite so there's blood; who keeps learning the games we play as quickly as I can change the rules; who can make me happy and I do not wish to be happy, and yes I do wish to be happy. . . . who tolerates,

which is intolerable; who is kind, which is cruel; who understands, which is beyond comprehension. . . ."

It is toward this exposition of a distinctive sexual relationship that the whole of my present study has tended. In her account
of George, Martha provides the definitive formulation of the sexual aspect of that love described earlier by St. Paul in *Corinthians:*
the love which is "slow to lose patience," seeks to be "constructive," and "is not possessive." It might seem strange to praise
George for forbearance after all the dreadful things he says (even
if he hardly *does* anything), but I have already suggested that
many of these insults are jocular, or ironic, or softened by a recog-
nizable context of affection. And he can be surprisingly scru-
pulous when he is being judicial. He apologizes instantly after
slandering some colleagues: "No . . . that's not fair." Moreover,
while George throughout the play is closer to failure and breakdown than normal (which is what makes for drama), yet by
extraordinary mental agility he never irredeemably loses control
of himself and the situation. Seen in the light of Shakespeare's
comic catharsis of the romantic misjudgments of figures like
Katharina, Bassanio, and Claudio, we may even see in George's
performance an example of the use of sexual shock therapy on
the other characters, for the reason why Albee's play is so exhilarating is in part that it is a true comedy: all the characters finish
better off than they were when the play started. That they do so
is largely attributable to George.

My students find the same difficulty in recognizing the piv-
otal virtue of figures like George as Chinese aristocrats traditionally did in identifying sages. Chinese folklore is full of stories
of princes going to visit wise men for advice and discovering on
arrival that they have already crudely misused the inconspicuous
sage when they encountered him on the road, because his wisdom
insured his near invisibility among ordinary people. Shakespeare's
fool in *King Lear* has this characteristic, as does Pierre Bezukhov
in Tolstoy's *War and Peace* (many Russian authors exploit the

effect, particularly Chekhov in his plays and Dostoevsky in *The Idiot*). In the case of George this inconspicuousness is so marked that it helps to relate him to Petruchio, as the moon allusion invites us to do. Like Petruchio, George has to cope with a powerful but neurotic personality in his wife. Like Katharina, Martha has at least once physically attacked her husband and even managed to lay him out cold. She makes all the crude attempts to achieve maleness which are also a defect in Cleopatra; Martha even makes exactly the same claim to superiority over George that the Egyptian queen does over Antony: "Look, sweetheart, I can drink you under any goddam table you want"; and they both use the same transvestite symbolism: "I wear the pants in this house." Indeed, Martha duplicates Cleopatra's tendency to play the all-encompassing role of Isis: "You're all flops. I am the Earth Mother, and you're all flops."

Martha is obviously the inheritor of an excessively imaginative view of sex; as George says: "Martha's a Romantic at heart." At her first appearance she is busy trying to identify with Bette Davis in a "Warner Brothers epic." Later we hear that her first sexual adventure with a "naked" gardener was as literary, in modern terms, as Romeo was in Petrarchan ones: "a kind of junior Lady Chatterley arrangement, as it turned out." She even admits of George himself that she "actually fell for him." It is not surprising to hear George assert that she spends time in rest homes, though he later says only that she needs to rather than that she actually has. But her instability is corroborated by frequent comment about her fixation on her aloof, unloving father: "Mommy died early, see, and I sort of grew up with Daddy. . . . Jesus, I admired that guy! I worshipped him . . . I absolutely worshipped him. I still do. And he was pretty fond of me, too . . . you know? We had a real . . . rapport going." George skillfully deflates this enduring Oedipus complex, first by ridicule: "Your father has tiny red eyes . . . like a white mouse. In fact, he *is* a white mouse." Finally he uses the decisive weapon of therapeutic shock in asserting that in fact she has "a father who really doesn't give a damn whether she lives or dies, who couldn't care less *what* happens to his only daughter." Certainly Martha has comparable descriptions of George's personality as neurotic; but somehow we never discover whether the grossly Oedipal plot of George's novel is really autobiographical. Martha's level of response is always cruder than George's, more destructive, less creative. Even her revenges are self-betrayals: "I'll make you sorry you made me want to marry you." She herself admits her destructive potential: "Some day . . . hah! some *night* . . . some stupid, liquor-ridden night . . . I will go too far . . . and I'll either break the man's back . . . or push him off for good . . . which is what I deserve."

The play deals with the moment when her neurotic energy and emotional extremism come as close as possible to this, only for George's virtuosity to redeem it to their mutual advantage. She has abused him more sweepingly than ever before, and he uses the energies generated by her betrayals as a means of cleansing their life of one more pathological fiction: the fantasy about their having a son. Obviously, he has developed this fiction to compensate for their childlessness, but he decides that her aggressive self-esteem (witness the Earth Mother routine) is verging on megalomania, and he is now able to drive out one neurosis by simultaneously collapsing another. He uses a farcical manner to destroy their child myth (he "eats" the supposed telegram announcing their son's "death," in order to explain its disappearance). The ridiculous effects involved finally reduce Martha to the recognition that she is no goddess but childless and a rejected daughter, incapable of inducing an orgasm even in a healthy young male like Nick. Albee requires us to face this condition as the plausible termination of a romantic view of sex.

Many may consider this development in Martha a loss of distinction, just as they prefer the grandeur of mad Lear to his humility when he finally recognizes himself to be "a very foolish fond old man . . . not in my perfect mind" (IV. vii. 60 ff.). But the insignificant-sounding sage is certainly preferable to the flamboyantly hysterical hero or heroine. By the end of *Virginia Woolf,* Martha has shown us her tremendous vitality and her power to respond profoundly to George, but she has also frankly, even publicly, faced some terrible truths about herself: above all that she is sterile and that George is not only the best man she's ever going to get but one she is lucky to have. The plausible portrayal of her assimilation of these painful truths is very moving. Compared with the supposedly life-affirming soliloquy of Molly Bloom at the end of Joyce's *Ulysses,* Martha's self-recognition seems like Christian humility; Molly's sexual fantasies have all the fatal hubris from which Martha has so barely been rescued. Molly is even then planning the seduction of the young intellectual, Stephen Dedalus, and sneering at her husband. Of course, for an acid person like Joyce even his heroine's acceptance of the guilt of her adultery and the insignificance of her husband is a considerable moral achievement, but it does not compare to the depth of self-recognition that Albee requires of his aging heroine and proposes for the contemplation of his audience.

The play cuts deeper than the novel, for all the richness of *Ulysses'* verbal texture. It also has great verve and a greater comic complexity. Its range of cultural allusion is as broad as Joyce's; it is necessarily more economical, definitive, and accessible than a novel, just because it is a sound play, and its plot structure is a consummate piece of virtuosity. Its two marriages are as beautifully interrelated and corroborative in intent as the endless juxtapositions which Shakespeare sets up in *Much Ado* between his two diverse couples. Benedick and Beatrice display the maturity which they have previously attained through bitterness such as Claudio and Hero experience before our eyes. Similarly, George and Martha subtly prefigure in their account of their youth some of the professional and sexual tensions of Nick and Honey.

However, Albee takes a more optimistic view of humanity than Shakespeare's, for his younger people are shown to learn from the sufferings of their seniors without having to duplicate them completely, something which Shakespeare does not show us in his comedies. Only in his last works can someone like Prospero manage to instruct Miranda and Ferdinand by a performance such as George and Martha's. Shakespeare's earlier comedies always show us youth largely incapable of learning from performances like *Pyramus and Thisbe,* and only to be taught by such agonizing approximations to disaster and death as Bertram and the two Claudios suffer. In Nick's new humility and Honey's acceptance of the need for children, not to mention Martha's own confrontation of the full truth about her life, we find plausible grounds for assent to George's flat assertion: "It will be better." If anyone in the play has made that possible it is he.

Albee's *Virginia Woolf* shows that Shakespeare's conception of sexual relations can be plausibly transposed into modern terms, and with particular effectiveness in a work generally recognized as a sophisticated and "advanced" play. This in turn suggests the falseness of literary studies which deny the creative relevance of the past to the present. The reasons offered for literary excellence in the modern world are frequently spurious, whether applied to the best contemporary writing or to works as old as Shakespeare's. Contemporary analyses of Shakespeare too often project back on him only the prejudices, if not the apathy, cynicism, and aimless complexity characteristic of many of the most sophisticated modern minds. But few readers are interested in authors like Shakespeare merely for antiquarian reasons. They read such authors at best as they read many modern ones, for a corrective vision of the present, some of whose virtues the older authors may have helped to formulate; so that a contemplation of their works may yet help to preserve and extend our understanding of the best potentialities of our own age.

CHAPTER SIX

The Self as Work of Art

H O W can one resynthesize Occidental experience for minds
to which it is scarcely more immediate than that of the
Hittites or the T'ang Dynasty? There are certainly wraiths of the
lore of earlier generations faintly visible in America today. A few
Jewish students have a mild interest in recent books showing that
the New Testament is just a well-intentioned fraud, and my
Catholic students often rather like the pseudo-Christian science
fiction of C. S. Lewis; but neither group has ever bothered to
read Plato or Machiavelli, let alone the Bible, though they continue to think of themselves as "students of the humanities."
However, they do have one set of ideas from which it may be
possible to work out toward such exotic concepts as Calvin's
ideas about original sin, Platonic Eros as the antithesis of Christian agape, or the sociological dangers of the Gnostic heresy as
reincarnated in the elitism of American academic intellectuals.
This shared set of ideas derives from the Freudian theory of personality. Though it needs some agility to transpose the Platonic system, Aristotelian categories, the doctrine of the Trinity, Hobbesian
political theory, and Yeats's masks all into the simple terminology
of Freudianism, it can be done.

However, initially the most my students usually have in
the way of a sense of personality derives from some vague memo-
ory of their divorced aunt's Freudian analysis. Even Jungian psy-

chotherapy is largely unfamiliar. The result is that many assume that human personality is a necessarily fixed and eternal structure, unless it is aided by professional therapy. Freud said you were set at five years old, and that is that. A dissenter often feels like Galileo challenging Ptolemy's astronomy, since Freudianism is the last orthodoxy to which people cling, with consequently heightened desperation. And in the case of someone teaching Shakespeare, there is a further complication. In view of his social conservatism, Freud found the idea that an upstart like Shakespeare should show such psychological insight in his plays distasteful. Only a man with proper academic qualifications like Bacon, or as socially eminent as the Earl of Oxford, could properly possess the sophistication to write the plays "mistakenly" ascribed to Shakespeare. In a mere bourgeois versifier such insights might otherwise suggest that normal middle-class personality really was supple enough to be capable of some adjustment without the aid of a professional analyst.

Recently, however, Communist Chinese techniques of brainwashing have helped a little to soften Americans' sense of the rigidity of personality, as has the transformation of negroes to Blacks. Novels like Hesse's *Steppenwolf,* and *Cards of Identity* by Nigel Dennis, have given the idea of easy personality change some fashionable aesthetic precedents, and the universal use of drugs has made it socially acceptable at least on a temporary basis. The main trouble with these experiments is that if you have only your knowledge of downtown Burbank to draw on, even LSD may only make you briefly the most unusual young man in downtown Burbank, and this may not rate very high on a scale including the lives of St. Francis, Chuang Tzu, or Pascal. My aim here is to suggest an alternative to present-day shock therapy as a mode of personality development for the intellectually gifted. As a device for catharsis, the use of drugs, sex, and speed (in all senses) is roughly equivalent to the use of a frontal lobotomy for the same purpose. At very least one might try those simpler, less dangerous devices of solitude or a little hunger favored by most expert mystics in the past.

Even these seem a little crude and melodramatic, implying a view of the inflexible nature of personality akin to the neomedieval theology which Freud founded on the assertion of the existence of a dangerous Unconscious, a lurking Demon which by definition cannot be recognized by its victim, and which needs the emotionally blasting techniques of a Freudian analysis to disarm it. As a religious ethic this may do for Portnoy and his fellows, but it is too clumsy and costly for most of us. If there is to be an adequate alternative view of personality change I would like to see it prefigured in Joseph Conrad's novel *The Arrow of Gold*. Conrad describes how the as yet unproductive narrator of the novel is judged by his fellow artists, one of whom generously puts up a defense for their naive victim to the other sophisticates: "That fellow is a primitive nature, but he may be an artist in a sense. He has broken away from his conventions. He is trying to put a special vibration and his own notion of color into his life, and perhaps even to give it a modelling according to his own idea. And for all you know he may be on the track of a masterpiece; but observe: if it happens to be nobody will see it. It can be only for himself. And even he won't be able to see it in its completeness except on his deathbed. There is something fine in that."

It is this sense of the possibility of some deliberate reconstruction of one's identity which lies behind my admiration for Shakespeare's portrayal of his most impressive lovers, and his criticism of his most disastrous ones. Biron, Rosalind, Helena, and Cleopatra are in no sense improbably aloof intellects as are Prospero and other mature "manipulators" in the plays. They are victims of desire and often afflicted by the course of their loves. But they are shown using to the full their margins of free will and initiative in the pursuit of a viable sexual relationship. This is precisely what Romeo and Othello fail to do. For them love becomes a completely revealed religion, or a psychological imperative, so that they appear Freudian puppets manipulated by a kind of Shavian life-force. As puppets they are inflexible, and under pressure they break. Romeo is thus one of the worst models to hold up to adolescents as an ideal. Biron, by contrast, could hardly be bettered as an example of creative accommodation to reality, as distinguished from the mere adjustment imposed on Bassanio or Bertram.

For if self-creation is an art, it may also be one full of hazards and difficulties, not the least of which is one's inevitable exaggeration of the autonomy of the self and an underestimation of one's conditioning. When a baby trips up by running too fast he first looks at his parents to see whether he is supposed to cry, or even perhaps to see how intensely he should feel the pain. Tolerable pain thresholds are socially defined and vary extraordinarily in different societies, eras, and situations, as American combat experience in the Vietnamese war has recently shown. Absolute emotional imperatives are so few that they do not uniformly govern human responses to the extremes of desire, suffering, and death in differing societies. Very few of our responses are truly self-initiated. A modern sociologist like Erving Goffman can even argue that there is no individual self distinct from the fluctuating roles that human nature assumes: "role distance is almost as much subject to role analysis as are the core tasks of roles themselves." In other words, detachment from socially accepted norms of behavior is itself a socially defined norm.

Indeed we may need to reflect our mental image in our own thoughts even more than in our physical appearance and behavior. The ultimate result of such a subjective performance appears to be the possible evaporation of any authentic self. This possibility leaves us in the ridiculous situation of never being really sure whether we are in any ultimate sense the people who we think we are or just minor variants of popular archetypes; and we have no certain way to make sure. When we "fall in love" with someone, can we ever be sure that we are not unknowingly surrender-

ing ourselves to the conventional diversion of affecting to have
fallen in love, a recreational mode of behavior which many societies have found it quite unnecessary to develop in their sex
lives? Such a view of the purely conventional nature of romantic
love would serve to explain Shakespeare's acceptance of the wil-
fulness of sentimental lovers' behavior: if startled they may easily
forget their affected role or be jolted into another equally artificial
one. Thus neither Othello's love nor his hate for Desdemona derives inescapably from his situation; he merely believes that they
do. His difficulty lies in his lack of any sense of varying options
at moments of crisis.

Shakespeare's comic vision of stage personality at least provides us with an immediate escape from the total evaporation of
the self. We may resist any denial of our autonomy instinctively,
but at a given instant we cannot prove that our actions are not
largely conditioned by a subconscious need to conform to a pattern of behavior which has been imposed on our nature rather
than being a conscious realization of it. The ethical consequence
of this uncertainty must clearly be the skeptical view of the self
suggested by St. Paul and illustrated by Shakespeare. Role playing may be almost universal and inescapable, but if it cannot certainly be avoided its dangers can at least be anticipated. Since
one cannot be fully sure of his own integrity, he must first systematically avoid any actions in fulfillment of one role which cannot be reversed if that role should later need to be modified to
suit an evolved identity. Othello may properly play the role of
jealous husband for all it is worth: rage, curse, insult his wife. But
he should not kill in sustaining the part, simply because that action makes him incapable of adaptation to later roles which may
prove necessary to justify or enrich his continued performance.
By committing an action which cannot be offset adequately later
he prevents himself from changing mentally. His mistake lies not
in being jealous (which is rather exciting), but in establishing
inflexible material circumstances to match this merely transitory

mental role. The same mistake of self-limitation is made in Macbeth's surrender to an evanescent mood of murderous ambition.

The professional discipline of acting has the philosophic merit that it trains one to play a thoroughly convincing role without ever being trapped in a binding physical action. The actor playing Othello does not actually kill the actress playing Desdemona. Playing the part of Romeo does not require of one that he physically impregnate the performer of Juliet's role or even share her bed. Thus Stanislavski's method acting initiated a modern attempt to surrender totally to one's role which is both a total violation of professional discipline and a repudiation of the only moral discriminations compatible with modern social psychology. Since it is unwise to surrender undiscriminatingly to any actual pattern of behavior in real life, it is even more ridiculous to invite any surrender to the adequacy of an admittedly artificial dramatic creation. Dr. Johnson carries such modern thought with him in asserting that in the theater "it is false that any representation is mistaken for reality." The power of drama does not lie in our belief that stage lovers are actually copulating or that real suffering occurs: "It is credited, whenever it moves, as a just picture of a real original; as representing to the auditor what he would himself feel, if he were to do or suffer what is there feigned."

The defect in Johnson's analysis lies only in his being unaware of how fully relevant the imitation is to the "real original." Obviously it is not so much that one might specifically behave in love exactly like Romeo or Othello as that one might make their more profound mistake of thinking that their own personalities are an adequate basis for any definitive action. The most obvious illustration would be the killing of someone, for death is something so irreversible that it can never be inflicted with propriety by the authority of a single personality on another human being or even on oneself. Whenever this occurs in drama or in life, it must heighten our sense of the inadequacy of any act founded on a basis as changeable as individual human character. It follows that any other kind of unqualified personal commitment, in life or on stage, also approaches fatuousness to the extent that it fosters enthusiasm for drastic and irreversible action. This is not to reject all drastic action but to stress the need to approach it with Hamlet's protracted analysis and almost intolerable procrastination, and to accomplish it with the reluctance, disgust, and self-hatred of Queen Elizabeth finally signing the death warrant of Mary Stuart for her ministers, or Governor Brown assenting to the state machinery ordaining the execution of Chessman. The propriety of such executions may still be resisted, but no one could complain that by the end of their vacillations the principal agents in these cases were naive or deceived about the objective issues involved, as are most advocates of punitive death or destruction, whose self-confidence is usually superior to mere facts and the considered advice.

If I often seem to have treated the best characters in Shakespeare's comedies as if they were real people, it is thus because the personae filled out by the mind of a Shakespeare are often more rewarding as models for life than the stereotyped personalities actually but unknowingly adopted by the people one meets outside the theater. Unfortunately, naive political commitment is reducing the power of the theater everywhere to project that awareness of the need for detachment which is so characteristic of Shakespeare. The rise of the documentary kind of presentation favored by the cinema has also helped to diminish our sense of the artifice of personality. Indeed, the cinema is perhaps the single worst offender in reducing the modern audience's sense of the artificiality of much of life as well as of art. It continually gives the illusion of an actuality which must be fraudulent insofar as its contrivance is not openly avowed. Its attempt at total realism makes it largely behaviorist in its treatment of personality, for it drowns any sense of the separation of the actor's own identity from his dramatic role, and in so doing it destroys the classic theatrical image of the real-life distinction between men's enforced social roles and men's attitudes toward these, in which alone any unique private identity must lie.

These aesthetic conclusions can be rephrased in sociological terms. If one knows from the start that a relationship such as "love" involves a great deal of merely diverting conventional acting and not very much truly metaphysical compulsion, one can take more conscious pains to play one's role skillfully and thus perhaps sustain it more successfully. We see that Bottom consciously playing Pyramus (however badly) makes for less of a tragedy than Romeo unconsciously playing his romantic "self," just as the actor consciously playing Romeo is likely to be a more sophisticated person than the routine victim of calf-love in real life. Mistakes of any kind are less likely to the extent that a lover's sense of his "performance" can temper his commitment without destroying its plausibility. In sexual relations as in any other kind one succeeds to the extent that one can copy St. Paul's extraordinary goal of "being all things to all men." His concern to convert others to his moral view is consistently tempered by a sense of the dangers of personal absolutism. As long as the relationship is not manifestly destructive he will respect any man's distinctive identity and its dependent world view. The worst punishment he will inflict even on willfully pernicious personalities is withdrawal, and he insists that his churches behave likewise: even recourse to law against sinners is denied to true Christians, whose harshest censure will be to avoid willful offenders. Paul's unparalleled success as a missionary to many lands is surely the result of this unique blend of commitment and flexibility.

The application of these ideas to modern sexual relationships produces some startling conclusions. The first and most important is that as long as lovers are not physically or mentally deformed, their individual personalities and attributes are unimportant in proportion as their love is likely to be enduring and meaningful, because only lovers skeptical of the substantiality of their own and others' personalities can possibly handle the complex interaction of subjective viewpoints implicit in any intimate relationship. If specific traits are unimportant, then all that counts is the will to adjust to another person (this really is the sole valid meaning of love). Granted the general recognition of the need for such an effort on both sides in any love affair, it is clear that any adept lover can mate willingly and successfully with any responsive mistress. As Donne says, "I can love both fair and brown, . . . I can love any so she be not true": only self-sufficient sincerity is destructive. Only a naive figure like Claudio will choose Hero for what he is confident are her merits, and then on the basis of the same values seek to destroy her. Learning wisdom, he finally agrees to marry unjudged anyone his friends propose and gets Hero back intact. After public shame, Bertram learns to be relieved that any woman will live with him, even the wife he repudiated so confidently. Beatrice and Benedick are supple enough to be able to marry even though each has proclaimed the other the most malicious wit in the play. Biron uses his ingenuity to justify his devotion to a sharp-tongued, pallid brunette who is ridiculed by his friends. Petruchio is cynical enough to marry even a shrew like Kate because he guesses that her need for love will serve to temper her harshness. Amatory sophistication thus has two distinct characteristics: extreme susceptibility to any plausible grounds of attraction when affection is available, and the deliberate use of intellectual power to recover this kindly posture toward the beloved in the event of any misadventure (even their spouses' entrenched hatred plausibly surrenders to such sustained commitment in Helena, Hermione, and Petruchio).

Young people are thus totally misguided if they look for "admirable" subjects with whom to fall in love. Unusual physical or mental attributes are of extremely short-term worth in love; indeed they are likely to be serious danger signals because they may well foster inflexibility and unresponsiveness in their possessors. As long as there are no positively inhibiting factors involved, awareness of the need for responsiveness is the sole criterion worth considering in a sexual partner. If one is not nauseated, any other limitations are unimportant; and this surely explains the extraordinary number of even severely handicapped people who have been deeply loved. Robert Browning married an Elizabeth Barrett who was practically bedridden. The authoress George Eliot, partner in another of the most famous Victorian love affairs, had a face like a horse. Petrarch may have hymned the divine Laura, but he actually lived in common-law marriage with a humble and illiterate peasant woman by whom he had two much-loved children. This kind of mundane reality explains why Shakespeare's Cleopatra seems so well observed. Like Falstaff, she deliberately pursues the skills of accommodation to an extravagant degree, and as a result, though she is in physical decline, she remains irresistible. Albee's Martha is another case in point: promiscuous, in her late fifties, neurotic, and bitter, she still obviously responds subtly to people, above all to George, as he does to her. Despite all their faults they are thus intoxicating lovers; dry as a martini but far more effervescent and palatable.

Shakespeare is the supreme master in the creation of such examples for us to emulate in the arts of virtuoso responsiveness, though he is closely rivaled by his adept imitator, John Donne. Shakespeare's plays rarely lack characters who display astonishing and salutary gestures of wry accommodation for our contemplation, as when the dying Desdemona exonerates Othello from her murder. These characters have sometimes offended critics. Many are incredulous when Lady Anne marries the hunchback Richard III, who has murdered her husband and his father, though that marriage is actually a historical fact. Perhaps the virtuosity of Petruchio or of Helena is indeed somewhat beyond normal attainment, but that of Benedick or Rosalind is certainly more a result of choice of attitudes to love than of an implausible virtuosity. If Diotima is wrong about true love in the *Symposium* when she defines it as an attraction to the exceptionally gifted, these norms for the sexual relationship may happily accommodate the talents of any of us who are willing to accept the single obligation that they enforce: the use of all our aptitudes primarily in the service of the relationship. As Donne is continually insisting, only ideals external to a love affair can destroy it. This of course is also true of any significant emotional bond.

The paucity of such enduring relationships in the modern world has led the young into a desperate pursuit of every simple goal which may induce the feeling of community. The loss of that feeling usually stems from the failure to apply E. M. Forster's aphorism that "people are more important than things." However, while this saying seems merely to indict the archaic American cult of material objects, it nowadays bears just as much on our modern ideological absolutism: to prefer the love of an idea to love of particular people is still to rate an insentient thing higher than a human being. A truly discriminating progressive like Ivan Illich speaks out most decisively against this modern variation of archetypal inhumanity when he says: "My real enemies are those who don't know how to laugh, who take things too seriously." They were always Shakespeare's enemies, too. Laughter is the only seasoning for love.

References

4. St. Augustine, *Confessions,* trans. R. Warner (New York: New American Library, 1963), p. 31; Ben Jonson, *Timber* (London: Dent, 1951), p. 36; John Milton, *Complete Poems and Selected Prose,* ed. M. Y. Hughes (New York: Odyssey, 1957), p. 694.

7. All references to Shakespeare's text have, for convenience, been keyed to Hardin Craig's one-volume *The Complete Works of Shakespeare* (Chicago: Scott, Foresman, 1951).

9. Samuel Johnson, *Lives of the Poets* (London: Dent, 1950), II, 392.

11. Norman Rabkin, *Shakespeare and the Common Understanding* (New York: The Free Press, 1967), p. 7.

27. Jonathan Swift, *A Tale of a Tub,* ed. J. Hayward (London: Nonesuch, 1949), pp. 334–336.

29. Plato, *Five Dialogues* (London: Dent, 1952), pp. 56 ff.

31-32. Clarendon citation from J. Dover Wilson, ed., *The Sonnets* (Cambridge: The University Press, 1967), p. cxx.

48. Andreas Capellanus, *The Art of Courtly Love,* trans. J. J. Parry (New York: Ungar, 1959), p. 100.

50. Plautus, *Six Plays,* trans. L. Casson (New York: Doubleday, 1963), p. 47.

52. *The New Testament,* ed. C. C. D. (New York: Catholic Book, 1949), p. 178.

104. 1 Corinthians, 13; in *Letters to Young Churches,* trans. J. B. Phillips (London: Collins, 1955), p. 79.

179. All references to Edward Albee's *Who's Afraid of Virginia Woolf?* are based on the Atheneum edition (New York, 1962).

184–185. Jonathan Swift's version, in *The Latin Poets,* ed. F. R. B. Godolphin (New York: Random House, 1949), p. 10.

199. Joseph Conrad, *The Arrow of Gold* (London: Unwin, 1919), p. 155.